TRUSTS

SUMMER

An anthology for
the changing seasons

Edited by Melissa Harrison

Elliott&Thompson

First published 2016 by
Elliott and Thompson Limited
2 John Street, London WC1N 2ES
www.eandtbooks.com

ISBN: 978-1-78396-244-0

Commissioning editor: Jennie Condell
Series research: Brónagh Woods

9 8 7 6 5 4 3

A catalogue record for this book is available from the British Library.

Printed in the UK by TJ Books Limited

CONTENTS

INTRODUCTION

If spring is all about looking forward, and autumn about dying back, summer surely is the present moment: a long, hot *now* that marks the sultry climax of the year. Roughly bookended by haymaking and the grain harvest, it is a time of fruition and plenty, of promises fulfilled. Spring's generative riotousness slows and ceases, and a stillness settles over the land.

For many people summer is a time of leisure: days at the beach, or picnics in parks and gardens; long, fair-weather country walks. Often it feels too brief, or comes in instalments: we pine for the six solid weeks of sunshine we believe we always had as a child. But in wanting to recapture those days we risk missing the days we still have – because what is that wish but a wish to be a child again, loosed from school, loosed from the house, and barefoot on the grass? Those elysian summers, polished to dazzling brightness by the flow of years, can never be recaptured; but we have this summer, however imperfect we as adults may deem it, and we can go out and seek it at every opportunity we find.

I hope this collection from The Wildlife Trusts inspires you to do just that. Like its companion volume, *Spring*, and the two that will soon join it, *Summer* features material submitted by members of the general public as well as new pieces by established nature writers, poetry, and extracts from classic works of literature. Here you will find glow-worms, and cuckoos ancient and modern; jaunts on sun-dappled rivers, and hobbies hawking for dragonflies; there are diving gannets and rare cliff plants; butterflies, sea-gooseberries, city gardens and the summer stars.

Haymaking and harvest are still key events for our farmers, but they're very different occasions now than they once were. No longer is the labour of a whole village required to scythe, rake, ted, pitch sheaves to the wains and build the ricks; no longer do women and children glean the stubbles after. Many communities are losing their connection to the land; our countryside itself has changed, too, no longer timeless but subject to alteration and loss. Summer is no longer what it was – not because we have grown up, but because we have lost perhaps half the wildlife we shared the world with when we were young.

It is not too late to turn things around, though, and The Wildlife Trusts are working to do just that. We can all play our part, by learning about the plants and animals we share the UK with, loving them for the joy they bring into our lives, and protecting the places where they live. Summer should be about abundance: it is our job to make sure we can hand down abundance to our children, for all their summers to come.

Melissa Harrison, Summer 2016

Now day by day, indoors and out of doors, the conquest of spring proceeds to the music of the conquerors. One evening the first chafer comes to the lamp, and his booming makes the ears tremble with dim apprehension. He climbs, six-legged and slow, up the curtain, supporting himself now and then by unfurling his wings, or if not he falls with a drunken moan, then begins to climb again, and at last blunders about the room like a ball that must strike something, the white ceiling, the white paper, the lamp, and when he falls he rests. In his painful climbing he looks human, as perhaps a man looks angelic to an angel; but there is nothing lovelier and more surprising than the unfurling of his pinions like a magic wind-blown cloak out of that hard mail.

Another day far-off woods in a hot, moist air first attain their rich velvet mossiness, and even near at hand the gorse-bushes all smouldering with bloom are like clouds settled on the earth, having no solidity, but just colour and warmth and pleasantness.

The broad-backed chestnuts bloom. On the old cart-lodge tiles the vast carapace of the house-leek is green and rosy, and out of the midst of it grow dandelions and grass, and the mass of black mould which it has accumulated in a century bends down the roof.

The hawthorn-bloom is past before we are sure that it has reached its fullness. Day after day its warm and fragrant snow clouded the earth with light, and yet we waited, thinking surely tomorrow it will be fairer still, and it was, and the next day we

1

thought the same and we were careless as in first love, and then one day it lay upon upon the grass, an empty shell, the vest of departed loveliness, and another year war over. The broad grass is full of buttercups' gold or it is sullen silvery under a burning afternoon sun, without wind, the horizon smoky, the blue sky and its white, still clouds almost veiled by heat; the red cattle are under the elms, the unrippled water slides under sullen silvery willows.

The night-haze peels off the hills and lets the sun in upon small tracts of wood – upon a group of walnuts in the bronze of their fine, small leaf – upon downland grass, and exposes blue sky and white cloud, but then returns and hides the land, except that the dewy ground-ash and the ivy and holly gleam; and two cuckoos go over crying and crying continually in the hollow vale.

Already the ash-keys hang in cool, thick bunches under the darker leaves. The chestnut-bloom is falling. The oak-apples are large and rosy. The wind is high, and the thunder is away somewhere behind the pink mountains in the southern sky or in the dark drifts overhead. And yet the blue of the massy hangers almost envelops the beechen green; the coombes and the beeches above and around their grassy slopes of juniper are soft and dim, and far withdrawn, and the nightjar's voice is heard as if the wind there were quiet. The rain will not come; the plunging wind in the trees has a sound of waterfalls all night, yet cannot trouble the sleep of the orange-tip butterfly on the leopard's-bane's dead flower.

Now the pure blooms in the sandy lands, above the dark-fronded brake and glaucous-fruited whortleberry, the foxgloves break into bell after bell under the oaks and the birches. The yellow broom is flowering and scented, and the white lady's bedstraw sweetens the earth's breath. The careless variety of abundance and freshness makes every lane a bride. Suddenly, in the midst of the sand, deep meadows gleam, and the kingfisher paints the air with azure and emerald and rose above the massy water tumbling between aspens at the edge of a neat, shaven lawn, and, behind that, a white mill and miller's house with dark, alluring windows where no one stirs.

June puts bronze and crimson on many of her leaves. The maple leaves and many of the leaves of thorn and bramble and dogwood are rosy; the hazel-leaves are rosy-brown; the herb-robert and parsley are rose-red; the leaves of ash and holly are dark lacquered. The copper beeches, opulently sombre under a faintly yellowed sky, seems to be the sacred trees of the thunder that broods above. Presently the colour of the threat is changed to blue, which soiled white clouds pervade until the whole sky is woolly white and grey and moving north. There is no wind, but there is a roar as of a hurricane in the trees far off; soon it is louder, in the trees not so remote; and in a minute the rain has traversed half a mile of woods, and the distant combined roar is swallowed up by the nearest pattering on roof and pane and leaf, the dance of leaves, the sway of branches, the trembling of whole trees under the flood. The rain falls straight upon the hard road and each drop seems to leap upward from it barbed. Great drops dive among the motionless, dusty nettles. The thunder unloads its ponderous burden upon the resonant floor of the sky; but the sounds of the myriad leaves and grass-blades drinking all but drowns the boom, the splitting road, and the echo in the hills. When it is over it has put a final sweetness into the blackbird's voice and into the calm of the evening garden when the voice of a singer does but lay another tribute at the feet of the enormous silence. Frail is that voice as the ghost-moth dancing above the grass so faithfully that it seems a flower attached to a swaying stem, or as the one nettle-leaf that flutters in a draught of the hedge like a signalling hand while all the rest of the leaves are as if they could not move again, or as the full moon that is foundering on a white surf in the infinite violet sky. More large and more calm and emptier of familiar things grows the land as I pass through it, under the hovering of the low-flying but swiftly turning nightjar, until at midnight only a low white mist moves over the gentle desolation and warm silence. The mist wavers, and discloses a sky all strewn with white stars like the flowers of an immense jessamine. It closes up again, and day is born unawares in its pale arms, and earth is for the moment nothing but the tide of downs flowing west and the branch of red roses that hang heavily laden and drowsed with its weight and beauty over my path, dripping its last spray in the dew of the grass.

Edward Thomas, The South Country, *1909*

Sumer Is Icumen In

Sumer is icumen in,
Lhude sing cuccu!
Groweþ sed and bloweþ med
And springþ þe wde nu,
Sing cuccu!
Awe bleteþ after lomb,
Lhouþ after calue cu.
Bulluc sterteþ, bucke uerteþ,
Murie sing cuccu!
Cuccu, cuccu, wel singes þu cuccu;
Ne swik þu nauer nu.
Pes:

Sing cuccu nu. Sing cuccu.
Sing cuccu. Sing cuccu nu!

[Summer has come in,
Loudly sing, Cuckoo!
The seed grows and the meadow blooms
And the wood springs anew,
Sing, Cuckoo!
The ewe bleats after the lamb
The cow lows after the calf.
The bullock stirs, the stag farts,

5

Merrily sing, Cuckoo!
Cuckoo, cuckoo, well you sing, cuckoo;
Don't ever you stop now,

Sing cuckoo now. Sing, Cuckoo.
Sing Cuckoo. Sing cuckoo now!]

Anon, 13th century. Translation by the British Library.

In late springtime the evening sun leaves a residue of light and brightness on sea, loch and river waters. Nights, still dark and starlit, become thinner somehow, and watery. Evenings lengthen, end-of-day airs are white and turquoise, amber and rose, insect-humming and bird-filled. Winter still lingers in small patches here and there on our tallest mountains, while sharp, wild weather systems blow in angrily from the Atlantic and test the strongest hearts, temporarily banishing spring with gales, battering rains and flooding. But in between these challenges, the earth continues to warm, sunlight is richer and wildlife responds with considerable gladness: birdsong is exultant, plant colours are vibrant, scents potent, creature business is determined and busy.

The yellowness of spring is steadily replaced by vivid greens. Unbridled growth is scented. First the sun-burnished bog myrtle, heady and intoxicating. Then a vibrant, sharp smell, like a new-mown lawn and so redolent of sugar and lemons it feels good enough to drink. All around the croft the green mantle, with sudden bursts of sap along stems and leaves, is responding to the call of sun and warming air. And through the rising scents push beetles, iridescent, dressed in black, turquoise, bronze, and in shimmering purples, reds and greens. Everything, it seems, like the larks ascending across the fields, is awaiting the sun.

Cuckoo calls echo across the valley in late spring, cocooned by the sinuous coastal hills here on the edges of the west coast. Their gentle 'cuck-oo' and harsher chortles are frequent for a few weeks, numbers bolstered by the great variety and density of potential habitats in fields, riverbanks, coastal machair, hill bogs and scraps of woodland. Little birds are busy, of course; they rise in cloudy clusters of song and chatter, squabbling and feeding, and draw in the larger hunters – raptors in grey, brown, white and gold livery swoop; furred and cunning night stalkers prowl.

Gradually the woodlands are becoming more shaggy and luxuriant. Leaves are opening with colour-shifting, wind-trapping, sunlight-catching, bird-sheltering and magic-making speed. Willow, with pale shimmering leaves. Birch, whose silver-purple bark is now hidden by cascading sap-green foliage that churns in the breeze. Spruce has new, teddy-bear-fuzzy emerald growth which looks velvety, good enough to cuddle, and not at all prickly. Scots pine, tall and stately, has thick, phthalo-green needles and up-thrusting, bright new growth, each finger pointing to the heavens like da Vinci digits, whose bases are decorated with rings of peachy florets, shooting custard-yellow spores into the atmosphere with every caress of wind or perch of bird. And mighty oak, leaves sprouting later than all the other trees, coppery-tinged and crinkly-still, waiting for full summer to arrive before proudly opening and turning rich green.

Meadow grasses at last begin to rise sunwards and croft fields slowly become studded by constellations of bright yellow buttercups, eye-bright white daisies and creamy clover. Like the myriad stars in a winter night sky in the north, they herald the approach of summer. They are quickly covered by fluffy-bottomed bumblebees who exude busy, buzzy joy as they work.

Along the shore the lengthening hours of light bring a new shimmer and shine to the landscape. Days are calmer, the sea glows and across the coastal grassland the delicious scents of growth, earth and life are in the air. Birds are busy, rushing to and fro, piping, whistling, trilling and whooping with parental determination, picking, sorting and gathering: fluff, grass, stem, frayed rope, dried seaweed for nest-building and architectural display. Though oystercatchers, bright-beaked and sharp-eyed, still sing songs of winter wildness and loss, ringed plovers gently whistle tales of sand and foamy seas, both nesting by stealth, hidden among the cobbles and pebbles of ochre-red Torridonian sandstones, green-grey Lewisian gneiss and white quartzites. Overhead the bonxies pass by, silent, hunting.

Although the land is warming, ocean waters are still very cold and generate sea mist, the *haar*, on windless days. Then curiously, as edges melt away and the sea becomes shore becomes sky, sands begin to glow in otherworldly orange. Waters rustle quietly in the gently breathing non-wind. Such stillness is intoxicating and infectious, and very curious. All along the shore birds gather, heads tucked, bodies still, predator alongside prey. The quicksilver sea stretches, horizonless, while overhead is white too, just a glimpse of pale blue here and there. This is an edgeland, a transitional, singular space, a place of magic and metamorphosis, a summer-in-waiting. As the tide turns the breeze begins to dance, waves awaken, slurping as though still thick and made of mercury. They begin to rise and then break scattering like star-studded fishermen's nets. A skylark rises first, calling out across the now-melting mist, the shore sleepers are roused and suddenly rush about as if caught red-handed mid-crime. Up they fly, soaring then swooping, calling out loudly until, in a matter of minutes, they are all, mist and bird, gone, and the sun is shining.

Nights too are shortening and lightening. The exultant dawn chorus is preceded by a voice, flawless and joyous. The song thrush, as summer approaches, extends the waking hours like no other bird; the first to rise, the last to settle, singing of life and growing things, of earth and sky, of light, warmth and joy.

Across the croft fields and along the riverbank in the calm mornings of late spring tendrils of whiteness remain in the damper hollows. The sun is warmer now, its former brittleness is liquefying. But on one windless day, the white mists of dell and sheltered shore seem to grow, not shrink.

Midges! Suddenly these sparkling midge-clouds break and then merge again like the murmurations of starlings. Then, diving through them, up and around, lustrous and spellbinding, are swallows. Higher and higher they soar, feasting on the wing in swooping, tumbling dances. Summer has arrived, at last, in the Highlands.

Annie Worsley, 2016

Cherry *Prunus cerasus*, a summer fruit. The early madock Cherry blossoms in March, the other sorts in April and May; the madock is ripe, on a warm wall, by the middle of June; the black heart, white heart, and Kentish Cherry early in July; the morella in August; the small black Cherry in July and August.

Thomas Furly Forster, The Pocket Encyclopaedia of Natural Phenomena, *published 1827*

It's only May, and yet it feels as if summer is well under way. I find it hard to imagine the woods in winter as they were just four months ago; now there is noise and activity all around. The long-tailed tits can be heard chatting again, and swallows are diving over the fields. The badgers are out in force, too: a patch of fading bluebells – or wood bells – has been trampled in the beech spinney, and a stampede line through the meadow grasses shows their route between main locations. The green barley crop now provides them with enough cover in the field – a small patch is already flattened. We're about to begin badger-watching again in earnest. It is my favourite month at the sett, for the cubs often put in an appearance and haven't yet learnt the ground rules: *Don't go anywhere without mother and always act with caution.* They will know soon enough, but for now we welcome their ignorance.

We settle in the field at eight-thirty one evening. There is a strong breeze but we're sitting downwind from the sett, so unless the wind changes it won't be a problem. Sometimes we stand looking into their wooded area, but nettles are shooting upwards and the elderflower branches drooping down with the weight of new growth, making it harder for us to catch sight of anything. That area won't see the full light of day again until November, so our only hope is that they'll come close to the fence, or up through their hole in the field to take a look.

Before long I'm watching one large cub come up and sniff the air just beside the fence. As expected, the mother is nowhere to be seen. The cub disappears down the tunnel and emerges into the field, soon followed by two smaller cubs. Once out of the ground they change their minds in unison and head back down the hole. I don't think they were frightened by us, but perhaps they smelt something a little different on the air, and their natural wariness is beginning to kick in.

There is no time to gaze off into the distance, as now a cub is ambling towards me. Has she really not noticed that I'm here? Her coat is in glossy, pristine condition, and she is without all the knocks and scrapes I'm so used to seeing on the older badgers – she could have stepped off a shelf in Hamleys, or from the screen of a Disney film. Her eyes are wide open and bright and she has a clownish tumbling gait. She comes within a metre of me, but then, feeling spooked, she runs away.

I don't like to come every night. I fear we may interrupt their foraging, and my own routine can't afford a nightly vigil. We stay little over twenty minutes, but see at least four cubs – more than many people will see in their lifetime. It is a privilege, but part of my reason in coming is to make sure all is well.

The footpath is turning pink, pale with chalk and lack of rain; the sunset is hidden behind a deep layer of cloud tonight, but some of its warm glow must be seeping through. There is still time to wander on; darkness won't come fully until we reach the village. On the way back I spot some blossom on the holly: simple white buds with a delicate blush, opening into four small waxy petals. I have never noticed its flower before; it bears no resemblance to the fiery winter berries. It reminds me again that each season is evident somewhere in the others, if only in the residue of fallen leaves, the dead seed-heads or empty nutshells. It feels now as though nature is racing towards the high point of the year, birds nesting, fruit growing in the hedgerows and trees, and young foxes, rabbits and badgers venturing further afield. Early summer is a time of nourishment and growth, not just survival. In some ways it saddens me that this phase is so brief – the longest day of the year is only a month away.

Caroline Greville, 2016

June

June 1.   Dames violets, double, blow finely: roses bud: tulips gone: pinks bud. Bees begin to swarm. Tacked the vines the first time. Began to plant out annuals in the basons in the field. Ponds & some wells begin to be dry.

June 2.   Sultry, & heavy clouds. Smell of sulphur in the air. Paid for near 20 wasps: several were breeders; but some were workers, hatched perhaps this year.

June 3.   Soft rain. Grass & corn improved by the rain already. The long-horned bees bore their holes in the walks.

June 5.   Boys bring me female-wasps. *Apis longicornis* bores its nests & copulates.

June 7.   Fly-catcher builds. Farmers cut clover for their Horses.

June 8.   Elder begins to blow. Many hundreds of annuals are now planted-out, which have needed no watering. Wheat begins to shoot into ear. Hardly any shell-snails are seen; they were destroyed, & eaten by the thrushes last summer during the long dry season. This year scarce a thrush, they were killed by the severe winter.

June 9.   Forest-fly begins to appear. Grass & corn grow away.

June 12. Drones abound round the mouth of the hive that is expected to swarm. Sheep are shorn.

June 13.	Martins begin building at half hour after three in the morning.
June 14.	I saw two swifts, entangled with each other, fall out of their nest to the ground, from whence they soon rose & flew away. This accident was probably owing to an amorous dalliance. Hence it appears that swifts when down can rise again. Swifts seen only morning & evening: the hens probably are engaged all the day in the business of incubation; while the cocks are roving after food down to the forest, & lakes. These birds begin to sit about the middle of this month, & have squab young before the month is out.
June 17.	Snails begin to engender, & some flew to lay eggs: hence it is matter of consequence to destroy them before midsummer.
June 20.	Cut my St foin; a large burden: rather over-blown: the nineth crop. *Libellula virgo, sive puella.* Dragon-fly with blue upright wings. *Footnote.* As the way-menders are digging for stone in a bank of the street, they found a large cavern running just under the cart-way. This cavity was covered over by a thin stratum of rock: so that if the arch had given way under a loaded waggon, considerable damage must have ensued.
June 24.	Hay makes well. The wind bangs the hedges & flowers about.
June 25–28.	[Bramshot] Vine just begins to blow: it began last year June 7: in 1774 June 26. Wheat begins to blow. Thomas's bees swarm, & settle on the Balm of Gilead fir. first swarm.

June 26. No young partridges are flyers yet: but by the deportment of the dams it is plain they have chickens hatched; for they rise & fall before the horses feet, & hobble along as if wounded to draw-off attention from their helpless broods. *Sphinx fortè ocellata*. A vast insect; appears after it is dusk, flying with an humming noise, & inserting its tongue into the bloom of the honey-suckle: it scarcely settles on the plants but feeds on the wing in the manner of humming birds. Omiah, who is gone on board the Resolution, is expected to sail this week for Otaheite with Capt. Cook.

June 28. [Selborne] Flowers in the garden make a gaudy appearance.

June 30. Wheat generally in bloom. The beards of barley begin to peep.

Reverend Gilbert White, The Naturalist's Journal, *1776*

I t was the first day of June, and the sheep-shearing season cul-
minated, the landscape, even to the leanest pasture, being all
health and colour. Every green was young, every pore was open,
and every stalk was swollen with racing currents of juice. God
was palpably present in the country, and the devil had gone with
the world to town. Flossy catkins of the later kinds, fern-sprouts
like bishops' croziers, the square-headed moschatel, the odd
cuckoo-pint, – like an apoplectic saint in a niche of malachite,
– snow-white ladies'-smocks, the toothwort, approximating to
human flesh, the enchanter's night-shade, and the black-petalled
doleful-bells, were among the quainter objects of the vegetable
world in and about Weatherbury at this teeming time; and of
the animal, the metamorphosed figures of Mr. Jan Coggan, the
master-shearer; the second and third shearers, who travelled
in the exercise of their calling, and do not require definition
by name; Henery Fray, the fourth shearer, Susan Tall's husband the fifth, Joseph Poorgrass the sixth, young Cain Ball as
assistant-shearer, and Gabriel Oak as general supervisor. None
of these were clothed to any extent worth mentioning, each appearing to have hit in the matter of raiment the decent mean
between a high and low caste Hindoo. An angularity of linea-
ment, and a fixity of facial machinery in general, proclaimed
that serious work was the order of the day.

They sheared in the great barn, called for the nonce the
Shearing-barn, which on ground-plan resembled a church with
transepts. It not only emulated the form of the neighbouring

church of the parish, but vied with it in antiquity. Whether the barn had ever formed one of a group of conventual buildings, nobody seemed to be aware; no trace of such surroundings remained. The vast porches at the sides, lofty enough to admit a waggon laden to the highest with corn in the sheaf, were spanned by heavy-pointed arches of stone, broadly and boldly cut, whose very simplicity was the origin of a grandeur not apparent in erections where more ornament has been attempted. The dusky, filmed, chestnut roof, braced and tied in by huge collars, curves and diagonals, was far nobler in design, because more wealthy in material, than nine-tenths of those in our modern churches. Along each side wall was a range of striding buttresses, throwing deep shadows on the spaces between them, which were perforated by lancet openings, combining in their proportions the precise requirements of beauty and ventilation.

One could say about this barn, what could hardly be said of either the church or the castle, akin to it in age or style, that the purpose which had dictated its original erection was the same with that to which it was still applied. Unlike and superior to either of those two typical remnants of mediævalism, the old barn embodied practices which had suffered no mutilation at the hands of time. Here at least the spirit of the ancient builders was at one with the spirit of the modern beholder. Standing before this abraded pile, the eye regarded its present usage, the mind dwelt upon its past history, with a satisfied sense of functional continuity throughout – a feeling almost of gratitude, and quite of pride, at the permanence of the idea which had heaped it up. The fact that four centuries had neither proved it to be founded on a mistake, inspired any hatred of its purpose, nor given rise to any reaction that had battered it down, invested this simple grey effort of old minds with a repose, if not a grandeur, which a too curious reflection was apt to disturb in its ecclesiastical and military compeers. For once mediævalism and modernism had a common standpoint. The lanceolate windows, the time-eaten arch stones and chamfers, the orientation of the axis, the misty chestnut work of the rafters, referred to no exploded fortifying art or worn-out religious creed. The defence and salvation of the body by daily bread is still a study, a religion and a desire.

To-day the large side doors were thrown open towards the sun to admit a bountiful light to the immediate spot of the shearers' operations, which was the wood threshing-floor in the centre, formed of thick oak, black with age and polished by the beating of flails for many generations, till it had grown as slippery and as rich in hue as the state room floors of an Elizabethan mansion. Here the shearers knelt, the sun slanting in upon their bleached shirts, tanned arms and the polished shears they flourished, causing these to bristle with a thousand rays bright enough to blind a weak-eyed man. Beneath them a captive sheep lay panting, quickening its pants as misgiving merged in terror, till it quivered like the hot landscape outside.

The picture of to-day in its frames of four hundred years ago did not produce that marked contrast of ancient and modern which is implied by the contrast of date. In comparison with cities, Weatherbury was immutable. The citizen's *Then* is the rustic's *Now*. In London, twenty or thirty years ago are old times; in Paris ten years, or five; in Weatherbury three or four score years were included in the mere present, and nothing less than a century set a mark on its face and tone. Five decades hardly modified the cut of a gaiter, the embroidery of a smock-frock, by the breadth of a hair. Ten generations failed to alter the turn of a single phrase. In these Wessex nooks the busy outsider's ancient times are only old; his old times still new; his present is futurity.

So the barn was natural to the shearers, and the shearers were in harmony with the barn.

Thomas Hardy, Far from the Madding Crowd, *1874*

June began with a storm in Bristol. The temperature was several degrees lower than average for the time of year and I certainly felt it, my skin exposed to the wind battering me over my handlebars. Trees shook, swayed and shed their weakest branches, littering the footpaths. My body was rain-soaked and tense from the brief, uphill cycle home and I soon regretted having mounted my too-small-for-me bicycle.

Unexpectedly, through the rushing of tyres on wet tarmac and shuddering exhausts, a noise pierced the city's soundtrack. In an instant I was taken away to deciduous woodland at dawn, away from the reality of dusk on the A37. I knew what it was. Perhaps no other bird would have the courage to perform a solo in the storm, nor have the power to produce notes that could compete with the roar of the traffic.

I've only recently come to appreciate the wren. Small and stout, this little brown ball bounces between bushes, pausing to probe with its needle-like bill, quite overlooked. I rarely spot them since they stick so close to cover, flying low to the ground and rapidly flapping short, broad wings. Every so often, I notice them rustling beneath hedges like mice, foraging for insects beside my feet as I pound along the pavement.

The wren is indifferent to our daily commute. Its pale, straight eyebrows give it a determined gaze as it busily darts between patches, relentlessly searching for food. Inconspicuous maybe, but although the wren is the most numerous bird in Britain, with over 8.5 million breeding territories, you are much more likely to hear than to see one. Calling from cover, this seasoned musician executes a rapid, cascading song from its narrow bill, finishing with a loud and clear trill. Despite the wren's tiny stature its voice is astonishingly loud.

Males continue to sing throughout the year, unlike many other members of our avian choir. If you close your eyes for a few moments and let yourself become aware of the sounds around you, you'll soon pick out a wren's song from the urban soundscape. Once you learn the tune, you'll hear it everywhere. That day, I was especially grateful for its notes as they carried me, through wind and rain, the last 200 yards to my door.

In stark contrast to the miniature, enigmatic wren, the city's most conspicuous residents produce the other sound you'll notice. Urban gulls are relatively recent residents. Since the 1970s, increasing numbers of both herring gulls and lesser black-backed gulls have set up home here. These large and robust birds are certainly not overlooked in Bristol, particularly in the summer months. Lesser black-backs have a slate grey back, and a fisherman's jacket yellow beak and legs. They tend to be a little smaller and slimmer than the herring gull, our quintessential 'seagull', snow white with a silver back, black tail feathers tipped with white, pale pink legs and the same bright yellow beak. Its call is a flamboyant affair. The herring gull throws back its head and emits a loud cackle, seemingly laughing at passers-by. Vocal birds at the best of times, during summer they are at their noisiest while defending their newly hatched chicks.

In contrast to the highly unfaithful wren, herring gulls are almost exclusively monogamous and can mate for life. Their success in the city is partly down to their urban parenting style. They choose to raise their young on the vast, flat roofs of tall office blocks, or perched atop Victorian chimney pots – both far from the reach of foxes and other predators. Despite an effective camouflage of mottled fluff, chicks are very vulnerable. Gulls are protective parents and we're a perceived threat.

The UK's breeding population of herring gulls has declined dramatically in recent years, though you wouldn't know it. Every summer the local papers report on the necessary pest control measures because, you know, gulls have been attacking beloved pets or whatever accusation has been levelled at them. Perhaps the negative reporting is not helped by the bird's mugshots, the steely look in their gold-rimmed eyes as though suggesting an intention to take over the world.

These attractive, intelligent and adaptable birds are resourceful opportunists that have learnt to profit from our greed. First following fishing boats and making use of wasteful discards at sea, then picking through our excess food in landfill sites, now they work as late night street cleaners by removing kebab leftovers dropped outside clubs and bars.

From my window I watched as a group of gulls soared gracefully above the city skyline, painting patterns in the clouds in a display of freedom. With the summer storm over and my bike safely stowed, I could clearly hear the soundtrack of the calling seagulls, which to me gives Bristol's maritime history a wonderful authenticity. I hope we learn to live with our wild neighbours before they move out for good. Not everyone has a nature reserve on their doorstep, but we do have miniature versions in road verges, playing fields, urban rivers and back gardens, as the presence of wrens and gulls gives witness. Summer in the city really can be wild.

Jennifer Garrett, 2016

Brilliantly fine and warm. Unable to resist the sun, so I caught the ten train to S—— and walked across the meadow (buttercups, forget-me-nots, ragged robins) to the Dipper stream and the ivy bridge. Read ardently in Geology till twelve. Then took off my boots and socks, and waded underneath the right arch of the bridge in deep water, and eventually sat on a dry stone at the top of the masonry just where the water drops into the green salmon pool in a solid bar. Next I waded upstream to a big slab of rock tilted at a comfortable angle. I lay flat on this with my nether extremities in water up to my knees. The sun bathed my face and dragon flies chased up and down intent on murder. But I cared not a tinker's Demetrius about Nature red in tooth and claw. I was quite satisfied with Nature under a June sun in the cool atmosphere of a Dipper stream. I lay on the slab completely relaxed, and the cool water ran strongly between my toes. Surely I was never again going to be miserable. The voices of children playing in the wood made me extra happy. As a rule I loathe children. I am too much of a youth still. But not this morning. For these were fairy voices ringing through enchanted woods.

6 June 1911

Wilhelm Nero Pilate Barbellion,
The Journal of a Disappointed Man, *1919*

It is raw here, even on an early June day. The wind races across the Narrows, the grey stretch of water between the island and Orford Ness. Beyond that, the North Sea brings white waves crashing on to the spit. But the sun is shining and I am cosy in my cabin although the wind beats around it seeking an entrance and sending the small wind turbine into overdrive. I can see an area of shingle from the window, gorse bushes, tufts of seakale, common gulls crouching low and one or two hares. They cower against the wind, wild amber-eyed creatures, huddles of brown moth-eaten muscle and sinew.

Havergate Island is Suffolk's only island. It is sheltered from the North Sea within the arm of Orford Ness that extends along the coast for about five miles. The island was walled off 500 years ago to keep the sea out and farmed until the 1930s. After the last inhabitants left it slowly reverted to salt marsh, lagoons and mudflats. It is now a bird reserve owned by the RSPB and accepts two volunteers a week over the summer to carry out species counts and maintenance tasks. I am staying as one such volunteer and have my own cabin.

I head out early to start the day's tasks as the tide seeps in among the sea purslane and pink thrift, flooding the salt marsh and the shingle path to Dovey's hide. The island breathes to its own rhythm. I wear boots against the wet. A few curlews trip along the island's eastern shore, unfazed by the wind.

Shingle protests underfoot. There are gulls everywhere wheeling on the gusts like toy kites in a frenetic dance. I am wary, keeping an eye out for the lesser black-backed gulls that circle, then shape to dive; it is not uncommon to get a firm kick in the back of the head, especially in the colony where the noise is a constant 'Yarh yarh yarh!' I tread carefully, keeping an eye on the ground as well as on the birds overhead. I negotiate shaggy nests of spotted eggs, some with downy, speckled chicks, taking care not to trample on anything living. The hares look on, forlorn, shifting about the edges like exiles, laying low in shingle dips and hollows or trying to hide in swathes of pink thrift and sea campion among the fragment bones of gorse, reels of steel wire, rusting iron cans.

At this time of year hares are still breeding, giving birth in hollow depressions in the ground. They have been here for who knows how long, waiting, suspended, as though the winds have cast them here. They tolerate the island and the island tolerates them. These hares have forever in their eyes. Eking out a meagre existence they shift about in search of shelter, vagrants in an uncertain world.

Today we paint the inside of the main hide. Trousers rolled up, splattered with grey, I inch across the floor, paintbrush in hand. Periodically I emerge to enjoy moments in the sunshine, noticing blue damselflies and red admiral butterflies flitting here and there, taking shelter where they can.

Evening, and the moon over Orford Ness is round and full, a warm, butter moon. Below, in its light, I can make out the dark shapes of fishermen casting into the rippling Narrows. The hares will be out feeding on grasses and herbs now. At night I sleep and dream reed-lined, silt-laden dreams, drifting channels in my skiff, hugging the shallows, calm and sheltered from a ravaging sea beyond. I wake and the winds are playing havoc with the wind turbine again.

The next day I count birds on the salt lagoons, shelduck, redshank, dunlin, sandwich tern. A group of spoonbills sift out small fish and crustaceans in the margins. It is a long session with little action on the bare, drawn-out mudflats that extend to the horizon. The pools shimmer in the June sunshine, but the wind chases across them rippling the water, puckering the edges and whistling through the seams of the hide. Mud and channels and a few bead-like shapes of birds. Soon my attention is drawn closer to the hide where, just outside in the grassy tussocks crouches a solitary hare sheltering from the wind, its right side lit up in sunlight. Haunches down, nose cross-stitched, it closes its eyes to the sun in a moment of blissful slumber. Close up it looks softer, smoky-furred and more relaxed. I watch it for a while as it sits motionless. Then it twitches, opens its eyes and sits up. It extends a foreleg exposing its whiter belly fur and patiently cleans, rolling its tongue slowly and methodically down the leg, paw buckled at an angle like a cat's. It has all the time in the world.

Later I learn that the hares suffer most in the winter, especially when storm surges from the North Sea breach the sea walls of Orford Ness and inundate parts of the island. Then the hare population can plummet. But it soon bounces back – the wardens are confident of that. In time, though, the sea will reclaim the island and there will be permanent losses. Birds can fly elsewhere when the sea comes, but the hares will be gone.

Alexi Francis, 2016

Of all bird songs and sounds known to me there is none that I would prefer to the spring notes of the curlew. I have seen the bird finish its notes on the ground after alighting, but I have not observed if it ever gives them without any flight. As a rule the wonderful notes are uttered on the wing, and are the accompaniment of a graceful flight that has motions of evident pleasure. The notes do not sound passionate: they suggest peace, rest, healing, joy, an assurance of happiness past, present and to come. To listen to the curlews on a bright, clear April day, with the fullness of spring still in anticipation, is one of the best experiences that a lover of birds can have. On a still day one can almost feel the air vibrating with the blessed sound. There is no rarity about it where curlews breed: it is to be heard through long days in April, May and far into June. In autumn and winter curlews resort to estuaries and the seashore, and the call note is melancholy: but even at this season on a mild day one may be surprised to hear a single bird give a few of the joy notes, just enough to revive memory of the past spring and to stir anticipation of the next one.

A yet more common and widely distributed pleasure is the spring flight and note of the peewit. It is a real joy flight accompanied by cries of joy: the seeing and hearing of it for the first time in the early months of the year are something longed for and welcomed, as is the first song of a blackbird. Some one in the wholesale trade in birds for food, explaining that pewits were of no use after an early date in the year, said, 'The birds are of no use after they have begun to *lap*.' I suppose, therefore, that the name lapwing is suggested by the joy flight in spring. At other times, the peewit gives an impression of plaintiveness.

The peewit or lapwing is a beautiful bird, much praised by farmers for consuming pests on their fields, but it has the misfortune to lay eggs that are an unrivalled delicacy, and these are taken in vast numbers for the English market, not only in this country, but in the breeding-grounds abroad. For many years I have not seen at Fallodon the vast flocks of pewits that used to visit us in autumn and winter, and which were probably composed largely of foreign birds.

The golden plover, when served on a dish, is so like the peewit in body that it can be distinguished only by the absence of the hind claw. When alive it is very different in appearance and flight. It 'yodels' very pleasantly in the spring. The call note heard frequently in autumn and winter is a single very plaintive whistle.

Redshanks in the breeding season have notes that may also be compared to yodelling; they utter these in a very conspicuous joy flight. Every bird seems to have something that is song, or corresponds to song, in the nesting season. Such is the 'screeling' of swifts as they fly about a village in the late evening; the conversational warbling of swallows as they sit on some perch or convenient place in the sun; wagtails have their little songs, and something of the sort is to be observed with all our common birds. One sound that was common in my boyhood has sadly diminished. The voice of the corncrake is now seldom heard in many places where it used to be common. No one can assert with truth that the sound is melodious; it is in fact very harsh; but it used to enliven many an early summer night in the field adjoining the garden at Fallodon, and I re-gret that it is heard there no more. Occasionally there is still a corncrake to be heard farther off, but both here and about the Hampshire cottage the bird has in my recollection become rare as a breeding species.

Two other common, but very peculiar, joy sounds shall be mentioned in detail. One is the 'churring' of the nightjar: a most soothing sound, continued for long periods without a break. No one unacquainted with it and hearing it for the first time would guess that the noise was made by a bird at all. It is of that class of stationary, soothing, continuous sounds, such as the hum a threshing machine, or the noise of waves on the shore heard at a distance, which dispose us to sit still and listen indefinitely.

I have not seen much of nightjars, but I had one curious experience, though not a joy flight or sound. It was evening, early in September; I had been sitting for some time at the foot of an ash tree that stood solitary in the middle of broad water-meadows. I noticed a bird fly from the branches above me, take something on or near the grass, and return to the tree. This action it repeated several times, and it took little flights about the tree. It was a nightjar, and I enjoyed the opportunity of watching it; for the bird was flying all about me and yet was unconscious of my presence. The bird was silent till at length in one of its flights it passed quite close to and saw me. So near was it that I could see it see me. It give a piercing shriek, such as I had never heard before from any bird, and flew straight away out of the meadow. For a moment when it discovered me its head had turned in my direction, and the shriek seemed to be uttered *at* me. It suggested not so much fear as rage and loathing: as if the bird was suddenly aware that, unknown to it, a human eye had been watching it, when it believed there was security and privacy. The wife of Candaules, when she knew that the eye of a man not her husband has covertly seen her disrobing, can hardly have felt more horror and indignation than was expressed by that nightjar's shriek.

Sir Edward Grey, The Charm of Birds, *1927*

It is a cool early summer's evening on a grassy hillside beneath a wood, and in the leaf litter beneath a bramble patch a small beetle larva stirs and sets off in search of what will be her last meal. Looking rather like an elongated woodlouse, her segmented charcoal-grey back is marked with pale yellow spots down either side and as she walks she repeatedly curls the tip of her tail under her body, pressing it against the ground to propel herself forwards. Even in the bright moonlight her tiny eyes are all but useless, leaving her largely oblivious to anything going on more than an inch or two away. Indeed her universe barely extends beyond the tips of her stubby but sensitive feelers, constantly twitching as she swings her head from side to side, touching and tasting her way through the leaves. Yet these are all the senses she needs to follow the trail of her prey and after several patient hours of hunting she finds her target: a large snail grazing lazily on a fallen leaf, its yellow shell banded with brown like a humbug. Undaunted by its towering bulk, many times larger than herself, the larva carries out the kill with surgical precision, gingerly stretching out her neck and using her hollow, scimitar-shaped jaws to deliver a series of delicate and carefully placed nips to the edge of the snail's foot, each time retracting her head to dodge any retaliation. Each bite injects a minute dose of a powerful toxin that simultaneously paralyses and tenderizes her victim. For a creature whose staple diet consists of slime-coated slugs and snails she is scrupulously clean and, reluctant to sully her feet by touching the snail's skin, she clambers on to the shell, clings to the rim and waits for the poison to take effect. The snail tries to flee, the larva riding on its back, but to no avail and when it finally succumbs the feasting can begin. Two hours later, when the larva finally abandons the empty shell, her skin is taut and bulging at the seams. She will not need to eat again.

Now she must seek out a safe refuge, a crevice in the soil or an abandoned worm burrow, where she can rest undisturbed as she prepares to enter the next stage of her life. Having chosen a suitable retreat she lies curled and motionless for two whole days before wriggling out of her old skin to reveal the pupa within. At first the surface is pink and yellow, like some sort of confectionery, but soon it darkens to a dull olive-brown. Another week passes in apparent inactivity, but beneath the surface her body is being completely but invisibly dismantled and rebuilt. Then one evening she will quietly shed her skin for the last time and emerge in her final, adult form.

When the last sunset colours have disappeared from the sky and the grassy slope beyond the brambles has faded from greens to shades of grey, the beetle makes her way to the surface and begins to climb slowly up a grass stem. As she does so a truly remarkable thing happens. From the tip of her tail a brilliant lime-green light shines out across the colourless hillside. She is a glow-worm! With neither wings to fly nor jaws to feed, her life has now become a race against time. She must use her light to attract a mate and then lay her eggs before the energy reserves that she had saved up during her two years as a snail-eating larva are exhausted and she starves to death.

Silently she continues her display: a cold, steady, almost unnatural light. Sadly her eyesight has hardly improved with age, and in any case she keeps her head hidden within a fleshy hood, so she will never know quite how beautiful she really is. If she is not successful this evening she will have to return to her underground shelter and repeat her performance the next night, and the next. But tonight she is lucky; within an hour she has a visitor.

With his large wings, protected by dark, leathery wing cases, he hardly seems to belong to the same species. Unlike her he has a pair of enormous many-faceted eyes, like two ripe blackberries, that almost engulf his head and allow him to spot the female's beacon from the air as he patrols the bank, so that he can drop down and land beside her. But like her he is unable to feed and time is too short for niceties, so formal introductions and courtship are virtually nonexistent. No sooner have they met and recognized each other by their respective scents than mating begins, the male's only nod to intimacy being the occasional gentle caress of the female's back with his antennae. Before long the pair are joined by another male, and another, all jostling and shoving, intent on prising each other from the female's back. Meanwhile she, apparently unimpressed, sets off back to her shelter, carrying her passengers with her. After two years spent pursuing snails and just one night of freedom, she will never again shine her light nor leave her den. By dawn she will already be depositing the first of her eggs, each glowing faintly in the darkness of the burrow, and within days of laying the last one she will die, empty and exhausted, never to see them hatch into the next generation of snail-hunters. This same performance has been played out over thousands of summers in countless meadows, woodland glades and hedgerows across Britain. The glow-worm's intense green light must surely rank as one of nature's most charming and magical sights, so bright that it is hard to believe that it could be made by any living creature, much less a humble, otherwise drab and unexceptional beetle. I still have vivid memories of my first childhood encounter with that light and even now, nearly half a century later, the moment of discovery of the first glow-worm of each summer is every bit as special, a small but treasured milestone in the passing of the year.

John Tyler, 2016

There is a slight but perceptible colour in the atmosphere of summer. It is not visible close at hand, nor always where the light falls strongest, and if looked at too long it sometimes fades away. But over gorse and heath, in the warm hollows of wheatfields, and round about the rising ground there is something more than air alone. It is not mist, nor the hazy vapour of autumn, nor the blue tints that come over distant hills and woods.

As there is a bloom upon the peach and grape, so this is the bloom of summer. The air is ripe and rich, full of the emanations, the perfume, from corn and flower and leafy tree. In strictness the term will not, of course, be accurate, yet by what other word can this appearance in the atmosphere be described but as a bloom? Upon a still and sunlit summer afternoon it may be seen over the osier-covered islets in the Thames immediately above Teddington Lock.

It hovers over the level cornfields that stretch towards Richmond, and along the ridge of the wooded hills that bound them. The bank by the towing-path is steep and shadowless, being bare of trees or hedge; but the grass is pleasant to rest on, and heat is always more supportable near flowing water. In places the friable earth has crumbled away, and there, where the soil and the stones are exposed, the stone-crop flourishes. A narrow footpath on the summit, raised high above the water, skirts the corn, and is overhung with grass heavily laden by its own seed.

Sometimes in early June the bright trifolium, drooping with its weight of flower, brushes against the passer-by – acre after acre of purple. Occasionally the odour of beans in blossom floats out over the river. Again, above the green wheat the larks rise, singing as they soar; or later on the butterflies wander over the yellow ears. Or, as the law of rotation dictates, the barley whitens under the sun. Still, whether in the dry day, or under the dewy moonlight, the plain stretching from the water to the hills is never without perfume, colour, or song.

There stood, one summer not long since, in the corner of a barley field close to the Lock, within a stone's throw, perfect shrubs of mallow, rising to the shoulder, thick as a walking stick, and hung with flower. Poppies filled every interstice between the barley stalks, their scarlet petals turned back in very languor of exuberant colour, as the awns, drooping over, caressed them. Poppies, again, in the same fields formed a scarlet ground from which the golden wheat sprang up, and among it here and there, shone the large blue rays of wild succory.

The paths across the corn having no hedges, the wayfarer really walks among the wheat, and can pluck with either hand. The ears rise above the heads of children, who shout with joy as they rush along as though to the arms of their mother.

Beneath the towing-path, at the roots of the willow bushes, which the tow-ropes, so often drawn over them, have kept low, the water-docks lift their thick stems and giant leaves. Bunches of rough-leaved comfrey grow down to the water's edge – indeed, the coarse stems sometimes bear sings of having been partially under water when a freshet followed a storm. The flowers are not so perfectly bell-shaped as those of some plants, but are rather tubular. They appear in April, though then green, and may be found all the summer months. Where the comfrey grows thickly the white bells give some colour to the green of the bank, and would give more were they not so often overshadowed by the leaves.

Water betony, or persicaria, lifts its pink spikes everywhere, tiny florets close together round the stem at the top; the leaves are willow-shaped, and there is scarcely a hollow or break in the bank where the earth has fallen which is not clothed with them. A mile or two up the river the tansy is plentiful, bearing golden buttons, which, like every fragment of the feathery foliage, if pressed in the fingers, impart to them a particular scent. There, too, the yellow loose-strife pushes up its tall slender stalks to the top of the low willow bushes, that the bright yellow flowers may emerge from the shadow.

The river itself, the broad stream, ample and full, exhibits all its glory in this reach; from One Tree to the Lock it is nearly straight, and the river itself is everything. Between wooded hills, or where divided by numerous islets, or where trees and hedges enclose the view, the stream is but part of the scene. Here it is all. The long raised bank without a hedge or fence, with the cornfields on its level, simply guides the eye to the water. Those who are afloat upon it insensibly yield to the influence of the open expanse.

The boat whose varnished sides but now slipped so gently that the cutwater did not even raise a wavelet, and every black rivet head was visible as a line of dots, begins to forge ahead. The oars are dipped farther back, and as the blade feels the water holding it in the hollow, the lissome wood bends to its work. Before the cutwater a wave rises, and, repulsed, rushes outwards. At each stroke, as the weight swings towards the prow, there is just the least faint depression at its stem as the boat travels. Whirlpool after whirlpool glides from the oars, revolving to the rear with a threefold motion, round and round, backwards and outwards. The crew impart their own life to their boat; the animate and inanimate become as one, the boat is no longer wooden but alive.

Richard Jefferies, Nature Near London, *1883*

Of the Solstitial Season perhaps it may be said that it is the most delightful of the whole year; for though the period we have just been considering is the most adorned with blossoms, yet the days are now attained to their full length, a beautiful twilight takes the place of night, and we seldom or never feel cold, except in particular unseasonable years. Besides this the air is generally calm and wholesome, and though sometimes great heat prevails, yet it is relieved by thundershowers, and the evenings are refreshing and delightful.

Full grown grass in the meadows, the flowering of the purple Clover, of the midsummer Daisy, of the Yellow Rattle *Rhinanthus Crista Galli*, and in the corn fields of red Poppy, mark the approach of the solstice. In our gardens the Scarlet Lightning *Lychnis Chalcedonica*, the Sweet Williams *Dianthus barbatus*, Pinks, and the whole of that beautiful tribe the Roses, besides numerous other plants, are peculiar to this season, and would be a certain mark of its presence to any botanist who might, after a long voyage, be shipwrecked without any almanack on our shores. Sheepshearing takes place early in this season. Dyer, in his Poem of the 'Fleece', says:

'— If verdant Elder spread
Her silver flowers, if humble Daisies yield
To yellow Crowfoot and luxuriant grass,
Gay shearing time approaches.'

The flowering of the Elder is a phenomenon of the early part of this season; the Hawthorn still continues in bloom, but the fruit trees are out of flower and the fruit set.

Most of the Lilies flower in this season, the yellow Pompoon is the first, the orange Lily follows; last the Turk's caps and the white Lily. In the early part of the season the major part of the species of Iris flower.

Some fruits are ripe towards the end of this season. Scarlet Strawberries come into season about the 15th June, the larger sorts before midsummer day; Maydock Cherries ripen at the same time, and the first week of July generally colours the red, white, and black Currants. [...]

During the Solstitial Season the interesting business of haymaking takes place. Meadow grass is generally cut about London by the 15th of June; indeed the haymaking of this district usually occurs between St. Barnaby tide and St. Swithin; in London's immediate neighbourhood it is usually over a week or ten days sooner than in the country. Milton, in '1' Allegro', well depicts the scenery and manners of a haymaking in the country, and gives us a lively and natural picture of its rustic festivities.

This season often closes with very hot weather, which gives place to the aestival rains during the ensuing season; the last fourteen days are called the Dog days.

Thomas Furly Forster, The Pocket Encyclopaedia of Natural Phenomena, *published 1827*

I f you've ever spent time by a freshwater river or lake then you will probably have seen mayflies as they dance gracefully over the water, skimming the surface and tempting the fish below to leap out at the chance of a delicious mouthful. These ancient insects have a 300-million-year history yet have barely changed since they flew alongside dinosaurs.

Mayflies have enchanted writers and poets for centuries. The philosopher Aristotle was particularly intrigued by them, describing mayflies as 'peculiar, bloodless animals', and giving them their original name of *ephemeron* or 'dayfly', meaning 'short living'. Like many others, Aristotle believed that this insect lived just for a single day to complete its one and only objective; to breed. In just one day they are born, they grow, they dance, they mate, they die. Yet however short their lifespan, mayflies have survived far longer than most species on our planet. Their basic life cycle is incredibly successful. For me, it is a joy to watch a horde of mayflies, erratically flying, buzzing around in different directions, simply hoping to bump into a mate, and in so doing, supporting a plethora of life year after year. They tell us about water health, and play a vital part in the food chain.

Mayflies are embedded in our history, folklore and literature. In Hans Christian Andersen's story 'The Old Oak Tree's Last Dream', the oak tree feels saddened that the mayfly's life is so short, with some species only managing a few hours as adults. Yet because mayflies spend most of their life in larval form, in reality they live for much longer. Depending on which of Britain's fifty-one species of mayfly larvae they are, the naiads or nymphs burrow, crawl or swim. Crawling naiads tend to be found in fast-moving bodies of water, their strong, clawed legs preventing them from being dragged away by the current. Swimming naiads prefer a faster moving river as this helps to propel them from place to place. Burrowing mayflies are an immensely important bio-indicator, as the nymphs are sensitive to freshwater pollution and their presence, or lack of it, gives an indication of the state of the water's health. Fishermen rejoice at the sign of them, as mayfly are great prey, particularly for trout; they have been used in fishing practices for hundreds of years, with even the Romans making reference to their usefulness.

When the nymphs do hatch, there is a feeding frenzy. Fishermen keeping watch on the insects' life cycle head to the rivers in their droves at the beginning of the mayflies' emergence as fish leap up, breaking the water's surface and launching themselves into the air, mouths agape in hope of catching a mayfly morsel. It is a spectacle for anyone to see.

After spending anything from several months to a few years in this larval form mayflies skip the pupal stage altogether. When the time has come, the naiad floats to the surface and emerges flat on the water, sloughing off its exoskeleton and emerging as a sum-imago or dun. After a short period in this form, the exoskeleton will then be shed for the last time as the insect makes its final transition into adult form. This process is unique to mayflies, as they are the only living insect which moults a second time after forming wings.

Adults emerge during the day, usually on the water's surface. This is a highly vulnerable time, as they must remain on the water while they wait for their newly formed wings to dry out. This makes them easy prey for other animals such as fish, frogs, bats and birds. The newly emerged adults are usually more colourful, with intricate markings and shimmering, glass-like wings. They swarm above the water's surface, their newly formed iridescent wings reflecting the sunlight.

After their wings have dried, they take flight. The males will begin to 'dance', creating huge, billowing clouds like smoke as they rhythmically bob up and down over the surface of the water, their two front legs outstretched, reaching out to find their life's purpose. Females will fly directly into the swarm where a male grabs her with his outstretched limbs, securing his mate. The females have no choice of partner and on occasions males will sometimes wait on top of newly emerged females to ensure they are able to fulfil their life's task. Copulation takes place in the air and impregnation is quick.

Mating is the sole purpose: shortly after the females have laid their eggs, the mayflies' life will come to an end, their bodies gobbled up by chancers beneath the surface. If they die en masse, then hordes of bodies can litter the bankside, turning the air sour as they decay. On the Mississippi river in America, male mayflies annually swarm onto land like a dense, heavy snowstorm and then die, leaving behind mountains of corpses several feet deep. The carcass piles can take days to remove and have been known to cause serious traffic accidents.

We might think that their short life is a sad one, but as the mayfly in Hans Christian Andersen's tale said, 'You have thousands of my days to live, but I have thousands of moments in which to be happy and joyous.'

Alexandra Pearce, 2016

The day is starting late in the Kinder river valley: low cloud drifts, lifts and then droops again; rain follows the airstream. Trees grown tall as they search for more light, swaying threateningly on shallow roots constrained by gritstone bedrock. Rain bands sweep over: fine and enveloping or hard and heavy, slashing and flattening the hay meadows.

The High Peak still has some mature hayfields, and at this time of year knapweed, meadow foxtail, yellow rattle, plantains and vetches all make focus points in the undulating seas of grass. The scent of herbs fills the air if the sun shines. Some of the grass lies flattened but uncut, and some is cut and mouldering in the rain. Here and there, some has already been mown and gathered: tram-lined fields show buff, pale and green where farmers are hoping there will be enough summer for regeneration and another cut. They'll need it to winter the sheep.

Somehow, the patchy hayfield hillside pattern matches the ewes hereabouts: some shorn, most – because of the late-lasting cold weather – not. Gobbets of shedding fleece catch the breeze, flying and tumbling and picking up moss until thistles hold them fast.

Meanwhile, the ragged ewes walk on, trails of fleece blowing in their faces, like a vain old man's comb-over caught by the sea-breeze off Blackpool Pier. Some ewes have moulted a whole flank and a glimpse of scalp-pink skin shows beneath the growing summer coat.

We've gathered some of the shed fleece and scoured it. Yes, real wool-gathering, just as in the origins of the sixteenth-century phrase. Meandering hither and yon, untangling the fleece, careful of the thistle spines as we walk to the next tress that catches our eye. Watching sheep at a distance, you wouldn't think they have their own scent, but a bag of raw fleece has its own bouquet – herby molasses and coal tar soap. Not that unpleasant for a year without a bath. When we've had the best of the summer and indoor pastimes prevail, I'll have a go at spinning this – either with the spinning wheel or with the drop spindle I've been experimenting with here at Farlands. I've some wool dyes to try too, but also some lovely dark fleece from a Zwartbles sheep, a Dutch breed with a gold-tipped dark brown-grey coat that comes up interestingly tweedy and flecked. I much prefer natural shades and colour variations to the homogenised synthetic yarns in the shops.

Later that week, another warm, dry afternoon after so many cold miserable days – perfect for listening to the birds' post-lunch tune-up while my friend Mary, who has been visiting, packs for her return home. Here, the lambs and sheep punctuate the bird-song as usual: hearing the ewe answer its errant lamb adds that 'all's well with the world' dash to the composition. I could easily drop off, but settle for closed eyes while I recreate the valley image from the sounds.

Until, that is, the sheep down the lane up their act: no longer are there gaps between the wobbly bleats and throaty mothers' 'mehs'; the calls overlap and take on an anxious tone. Sounds as if they're being moved. Yes, more lambs and mums joining in, along the lane we need to be driving down to catch Mary's train for Coventry where the nearest you get to sheep is the

Children's Farm, by the worked-out pit. The single track lane with drystone walls on either side. Time to investigate – lean over the five-bar gate, I think. The good news: they're coming up the lane towards and then past us. Decent sized, sturdy sheep, with broad backs like coffee tables, encouraged on by a sheepdog and the two young men we've been seeing working the farm across the lane.

There is a sea of sheep swimming past our cottage: the ewes have done this before and head the tide. Some are even a bit blasé about it and stop to nibble the roadside plantlife. To some, as always, the grass is greener on our side and they make determined efforts to breach the gritstone wall, but these are chunky beasts and don't have the jumping ability of, say, the smaller Ronaldsay breed. They also have handy steering devices: the shepherds take them by the horns to point them in the right direction.

We enjoyed the spectacle – rare for us, but just another day in the life of a young farmer. The sheep cleared the lane in plenty of time for us to get to the station, leaving me quietly glad that they had ground their droppings into the tarmac. Beneficial as it would have been on the allotment, sharing the journey home with a bag of sheep droppings might be taking the recycle mantra a step too far for this Marie-Antoinette.

Julia Wallis, 2016

It is now June and the Hay-makers are mustered to make an army for the field, where not alwayes in order, they march under the Bagge and the Bottle, and betwixt the Forke and the Rake, there is seene great force of armes: Now doth the broad Oke comfort the weary Laborer, while under his shady Boughes he sits singing to his bread and cheese: the Hay-cocke is the Poore mans Lodging, and the fresh River is his gracious Neighbor: Now the Faulcon and the Tassell try their wings at the Partridge, and the fat Bucke fils the great pasty: the trees are all in their rich aray: but the seely Sheep is turned out of his coat: the Roses and sweet Herbes put the Distiller to his cunning, while the greene apples on the tree are ready for the great bellied wives: Now begins the Hare to gather up her heeles, and the Foxe lookes about him, for feare of the Hound: the Hooke and the Sickle are making ready for harvest: the Medow grounds gape for raine, and the Corne in the eare begins to harden: and the little Lads make Pipes of the straw, and they that cannot dance, will yet bee hopping: the Ayre now groweth somewhat warme, and the Coole winds are very comfortable: the Sayler now makes merry passage, and the nimble Foot-man runnes with pleasure: In briefe, I thus conclude, I hold it a sweet season, the senses perfume and the spirits comfort.

Nicholas Breton, Fantasticks:
Serving for A Perpetuall Prognostication, *1626*

Of all the hills, cliffs and valleys that form the western scarp of the Cotswolds as they slip down into the flood plain of the river Severn, Swift's Hill must surely be one of finest. Laurie Lee made it famous, but the beatnik letterpress poet in Stroud, Dennis Gould, has done a pretty good job, too.

It is not easy to find Swift's Hill. Even those partly familiar with the Slad Valley may fail to notice the sharp right towards The Vatch as they journey up the B4070 from Stroud to Birdlip. Of course the road is winding. Of course it is beautiful, so beautiful, all beech cathedrals and fields gilded with buttercups. Sharp brake. Change to first gear, perhaps second, then go carefully as you navigate the dips and turns in the road, streams, fence posts, farm gates and barns, cattle and maybe even a badger that came to an untimely end on a dark night. Next, a quick right-left hook on to a gravel road. Not too fast and not too far now, either, certainly not past the quarry's edge. Pull up and park. Others might have reached the site before you – perhaps a lurcher in a distinctive collar, almost certainly a Labrador. But they'll go. Soon you'll have the hill to yourself.

Remember your light scarf; the wind always blows on Swift's Hill. Even on a fine summer evening; even as the harebells and bee orchids flower. Set off. The stiffest route to the crest of the hill leads directly from its base, straight up, starting at a forgotten apple tree in abundant leaf now, green fruit forming. A gentler course meanders round the back of the quarry, its exposed limestone betraying Jurassic secrets. But leave the ammonites where they are, guarded by the ash and hawthorn. Instead, take the more difficult path where the views will be better.

Do not be mistaken. This is not a walk to be made lightly. Breath will catch; calves will ache; if knees creak, they will do that, too. But at some point as you pause to rest and brush grass seed from your body, a great lungful of clear, sweet, summer air will excite in you the faintest tingle of freedom.

Keep climbing. At a certain spot, a path following the contour of the hill will cross your way, leading to a wood. Follow it if you wish, but you'll soon return to the course.

In the evening sky that shifts from blue to pink to deepening lilac, vapour trails mark the westward journey of aeroplanes overhead. Great metallic carriers guided by the jet stream shuttle passengers across the Atlantic. On and on they fly but here, on the ground at your feet, all of Stroud is laid out, shaken across the valley like the proverbial quilt: a log cabin of pasture and hedgerow dark and light, of triangulated wood and linear settlement. Beyond, the river Severn shines like quicksilver as it snakes south to Bristol. On the horizon, Wales.

It is still up here. The view is yours. If you raise your arms, you might imagine you could fly. Is your heart filling up? Does it feel as if it might burst?

Despite immediate appearances, the hill is not in fact empty. You are not quite alone. Look around. There are butterflies here, marbled white, meadow brown and green hairstreak. Moths are emerging for the night. And bats. An adder might be hidden in the quarry you left behind and buzzards could be roosting in that wood. A hare will dart down the slope when your back is turned.

To hear the dawn chorus one May morning would be sublime, but on this June evening swifts circle in the sky and – watch out! – here comes a swallow, as quick as lightning, skimming the slope for insects. In a few months they'll gather and fly south. You, too, are tethered to another place. We are all migrants now.

Come on. Get moving. Get up from the spongy bed, the grasses forming a crown about your head. Carry on up the hill before it gets too dark. It's tempting to stay in this spot but there is a second smaller hump to scale and lights are coming on below. You don't want to be out too late.

On and on, up and up. Watch the scarf on the windy gap and see how the vegetation changes in this little spot. Don't stop now – most of the hill is climbed.

Finally. There. Breathless. You're on top.

Vivienne Hambly, 2016

That rich undulating district of Loamshire to which Hayslope belonged, lies close to a grim outskirt of Stonyshire, overlooked by its barren hills as a pretty blooming sister may sometimes be seen linked in the arm of a rugged, tall, swarthy brother; and in two or three hours' ride the traveller might exchange a bleak treeless region, intersected by lines of cold grey stone, for one where his road wound under the shelter of woods, or up swelling hills, muffled with hedgerows and long meadow-grass and thick corn; and where at every turn he came upon some fine old country-seat nestled in the valley or crowning the slope, some homestead with its long length of barn and its cluster of golden ricks, some grey steeple looking out from a pretty confusion of trees and thatch and dark-red tiles. It was just such a picture as this last that Hayslope Church had made to the traveller as he began to mount the gentle slope leading to its pleasant uplands, and now from his station near the Green he had before him in one view nearly all the other typical features of this pleasant land. High up against the horizon were the huge conical masses of hill, like giant mounds intended to fortify this region of corn and grass against the keen and hungry winds of the north; not distant enough to be clothed in purple mystery, but with sombre greenish sides visibly specked with sheep, whose motion was only revealed by memory, not detected by sight; wooed from day to day by the changing hours, but responding with no change in themselves – left for ever grim and sullen after the flush of morning, the winged gleams of the

April noonday, the parting crimson glory of the ripening summer sun. And directly below them the eye rested on a more advanced line of hanging woods, divided by bright patches of pasture or furrowed crops, and not yet deepened into the uniform leafy curtains of high summer, but still showing the warm tints of the young oak and the tender green of the ash and lime. Then came the valley, where the woods grew thicker, as if they had rolled down and hurried together from the patches left smooth on the slope, that they might take the better care of the tall mansion which lifted its parapets and sent its faint blue summer smoke among them. Doubtless there was a large sweep of park and a broad glassy pool in front of that mansion, but the swelling slope of meadow would not let our traveller see them from the village green. He saw instead a foreground which was just as lovely – the level sunlight lying like transparent gold among the gently curving stems of the feathered grass and the tall red sorrel, and the white ambels of the hemlocks lining the bushy hedgerows. It was that moment in summer when the sound of the scythe being whetted makes us cast more lingering looks at the flower-sprinkled tresses of the meadows.

George Eliot, Adam Bede, *1859*

Mackarel *Scomber scomber*, appear in vast shoals on our southern coasts about midsummer. When first taken out of the water it emits a phosphoric light.

Thomas Furly Forster, The Pocket Encyclopaedia of Natural Phenomena, *published 1827*

The window is open and there's a distinct buzz coming from somewhere in the distance: a monotonous, metallic drone. Then another strikes up. This one stops and starts, as if someone was using a sewing machine nearby. We leave the house as though beckoned by the sound, to find it's the chirruping of Roesel's and great green bush crickets.

The British countryside has been transformed by new arrivals. It is the season when millions of birds come from overseas to mingle with the natives. They spend the summer foraging, mating and fledging. As well as the usual troop of songbirds, there are now water and woodland birds, well equipped to hunt in our waterways and skies.

Something flashes across the perimeter of my vision, a brown smudge that moves too quickly for the eye to follow. A crescent shape with a pair of compasses in its wake. Not the vapour trail of a plane but a small bird of prey, a hobby, which briefly settles on a dead branch before lifting off again and disappearing.

Hours pass. The sun is high in the sky. It's hot. Bees, dragonflies and butterflies fly back and forth among the vegetation. The hedgerows and reeds are alive with buzzing. Taking advantage of the industry of these insects, new hunters appear, a flock of over thirty hobbies filling the sky. Their gunmetal-grey backs and streaky underparts are drab. Their shape is slight but red tarnishes their thighs as if symbolising the many insects they'll eat over the course of one summer.

One of the hobbies descends and pauses, almost motionless in mid air before she lashes out with one talon in a kung-fu move. She is aiming for a dragonfly. Time seems to slow to a halt, as translucent emerald wings crumple like a sports car hitting a lamp-post. She clutches the insect close to her belly. As she re-joins the crowd above, she bends her leg and brings her prey up for mid-air examination. It's a southern hawker dragonfly, just right for a midday snack.

The sun is at its height. Summer is at its peak. The birds must make haste before the cold returns. At midday the air is warm and seems liquid. In the distance, a larger silhouette appears and heads for the lagoon, our second hunter to appear on the scene. He too wears the uniform of a bandit, a dark mask over his eyes. The harsh midday sun is bleaching the landscape to monochrome, matching the bird's own colours. He is an expert at long-distance travel: he doesn't have to flap but lets the hot air currents do the work.

Ospreys dive less often than terns or gulls, but more successfully. This star performer is a young male. He has already spent many hours practising nest construction. He is not yet ready to breed, but by next summer he will be and his nest-building skills will be put to good use. Now he has come to feed. He circles slowly over the water. For the creatures below the surface the shadow of his wings blocks out the sun itself. The blackness of his feathers seems to darken the sky. Eyes by turns topaz and dandelion yellow can see the whole underwater world, hidden from human sight.

Perceiving his chance, he plunges. His legs are outstretched in front of him like a long-jump athlete, and his wings are back and aloft. On impact, he seems to disappear into his own froth and spray. But he is no gannet or cormorant; he has not dived to the depths. Moments later he rises from the water. Clutched in one black talon is a fish, which struggles and flaps like a leaf in a gale. The fish, caught in the net of his toes, goes from flaccid to rigid and back again as it tenses and releases. It can't escape. Carried skywards, the fish's scales no longer gleam silver but become the colour of varicose veins and a muddy farmyard. Stress and asphyxiation make its eyes bulge and its tail jerk frantically.

Our hunter alights elegantly on to the same dead branch used earlier by the hobby. As the crest of feathers on his head stands proud, it is not hard to imagine this same feat being performed in the heat of the African sun. He picks delicately at his meal, one foot holding the fish flush to the bark, which begins to darken with a mixture of water and blood. He is using his other foot and his beak to tug at taut, stringy entrails and muscles until they snap under tension and come loose, free for him to swallow. He has the makings of a good father ready for next year, for in the world of ospreys (and of hobbies), good parenting relies on good hunting.

Matt Adam Williams, 2016

'**O**i' Way? Or 'Adventure' Way?

It's a choice that defines a person, and Eddie gave it his full attention. The canoe was in the water, and we had just scrambled on board, Eddie in the middle and me at the back so I could steer. Ahead of us the Waveney, gentlest of rivers, dividing – or uniting – Suffolk and Norfolk. Always seems to be slack water on the Waveney.

The promise of spring had given way to the achievement of summer. Unneeded extra layers in the dry-bag. First dip of the paddles and the stout, accommodating, infinitely tolerant craft came alive. But the question hung in the air: should we turn left or right when we hit the main drag? Turn right and we go through the pleasant town of Beccles – and crucially, under two road-bridges. These naturally give us the opportunity to shout 'Oi!', the call booming satisfactorily between the low roof of the bridge and the watery floor. This has an irresistible charm, and Eddie – my younger son, aged 14, who has Down's Syndrome – was keenly aware of the pleasures of the 'Oi' Way.

But turn left – up-river – and you leave the town behind. The river gets a little wilder between the tangled banks. Mostly we have the water to ourselves, and so we become a part of the wet wild world. I tried to keep my tone neutral, because it's only right and proper that Eddie made the big decision himself. 'Oi' Way? Or 'Adventure' Way? A world of understated joys echoing in that special word. Can Eddie hear them? We left the cut and joined the river as Eddie made the decision.

'Adventure.'

'Let's do it.'

We crossed the stream to hug the right bank, and at once found the right rhythm – the rhythm of the paddles, the rhythm of the river and the rhythm of life in the summer. That is to say, a certain lazy purposefulness. We were so close to the water we were more or less a part of it, affected by every gust, feeling the gentle tug of the tide and the river's movements.

The speed itself is a special experience: a little slower than an unhurried walk. But you can't stop on a sixpence as a walker can: you are committed to the steady movement through the water: observing what you see and hear with rather special closeness, but still committed to inexorable forward motion.

In June the warblers are still singing away, though less frenziedly than they did the previous month. I have counted seven species in an hour's paddle with Eddie; the sudden shout of Cetti's warbler and the lovely lisping descent down the scale from willow warbler are special favourites.

I remembered the words of the Water-Rat – Ratty – in *The Wind in the Willows*, as he told the Mole about the river. 'It's brother and sister to me, and aunts, and company, and food and drink, and (naturally) washing. It's my world, and I don't want any other. What it hasn't got is not worth having, and what it doesn't know is not worth knowing.'

And when you're on a river – *the* river as the Rat would prefer – in summer, when the livin' is easy, then no other world seems even possible. Sometimes Eddie paddled away like a good 'un, sometimes he rested his paddle at 90 degrees to our direction of travel and thought rivery thoughts.

No sound to trouble us but the birds, the cloop of my paddle as I performed my best J-stroke, and the bubbling run of water under the boat as we glided between each stroke with idle purpose. And then, on the inside of a bend where the water was at its idlest, as the plants make their stand in the shallow water, this slightly secretive little spot seemed at once to be filled with impossible, enchanted creatures. Clap hands if you believe in fairies!

What else can they be: for they were dancing, dancing in the air on wings that had been dunked in the same Quink blue-black ink that I used at school, but transformed into calligraphy more lovely than my pen ever attempted.

You see one, you see hundreds, for it was that kind of day. Time and again we came across another of the floating ballrooms and watched the dancers dance. At each dance-floor I told Eddie their name, and soon he had it for himself.

'Banded demoiselles.'

'Brilliant!'

Brilliant indeed: these were the males and their dance was the dance of life and death, a competitive choreography with the prize a gorgeous bronzy female and the opportunity to pass on their genes. They are related to dragonflies, though in these dancing frenzies they look more like a cloud of the most gorgeous butterflies.

To us passing paddling humans it looked like a show put on for our special benefit, but for the dancers it was the most important thing they would ever do in their lives: the thing for which all the time as a larva beneath the water's surface had been a long preparation. This was the Olympic Final: the time when all second chances have gone.

But all the same, how beautiful: the eternal gavotte of les demoiselles du Waveney. 'Shall we head back, Eddie?'

'Not yet.'

Another good decision, he was full of them that day. A little further on, a fizzing blue streak, low to the water, crossing right in front of our boat, giving Eddie the best of views. You know when you wave a sparkler in a circle on Bonfire night? You close your eyes and you can still see the track of its movement, burnt onto your retina. It's like that when you see a kingfisher. But blue, a blue laser streak inches above the less-blue water of the river.

We paddled back, navigating from ballroom to ballroom on the opposite bank as the dance continued. Soon, but not too soon, we would be in the garden of the pub, cold drinks and the river before us. Every season in the wild world is an adventure, but the gentlest and kindest of adventures take place in the summer.

It felt that day as if we could paddle forever.

Simon Barnes, 2016

Haymaking

After night's thunder far away had rolled
The fiery day had a kernel sweet of cold,
And in the perfect blue the clouds uncurled,
Like the first gods before they made the world
And misery, swimming the stormless sea
In beauty and in divine gaiety.
The smooth white empty road was lightly strewn
With leaves – the holly's Autumn falls in June –
And fir cones standing stiff up in the heat.
The mill-foot water tumbled white and lit
With tossing crystals, happier than any crowd
Of children pouring out of school aloud.
And in the little thickets where a sleeper
For ever might lie lost, the nettle-creeper
And garden warbler sang unceasingly;
While over them shrill shrieked in his fierce glee
The swift with wings and tail as sharp and narrow
As if the bow had flown off with the arrow.
Only the scent of woodbine and hay new-mown
Travelled the road. In the field sloping down,
Park-like, to where its willows showed the brook,
Haymakers rested. The tosser lay forsook
Out in the sun; and the long waggon stood
Without its team, it seemed it never would

SUMMER

Move from the shadow of that single yew.
The team, as still, until their task was due,
Beside the labourers enjoyed the shade
That three squat oaks mid-field together made
Upon a circle of grass and weed uncut,
And on the hollow, once a chalk-pit, but
Now brimmed with nut and elder-flower so clean.
The men leaned on their rakes, about to begin,
But still. And all were silent. All was old,
This morning time, with a great age untold,
Older than Clare and Cobbett, Morland and Crome,
Than, at the field's far edge, the farmer's home,
A white house crouched at the foot of a great tree.
Under the heavens that know not what years be
The men, the beasts, the trees, the implements
Uttered even what they will in times far hence –
All of us gone out of the reach of change –
Immortal in a picture of an old grange.

Edward Thomas, 1917

What country was I walking in, what age? Across the hedge there was a perfect Tudor manor, three storeys high, with two great brick chimneys standing as tall as a man above the stone roof. As I got closer I saw the house was hemmed in by caravans and that the road was thick with dust. There were no people, just the empty vans, ranks of them, and the house that stood as silently as if it were circled by snow.

The light was falling unimpeded now, in sheets and glancing blows. I wanted, like Laurie Lee, to stagger into a village and be revived by a flagon of wine. Instead, I tramped through the dust, dodging blue-black dragonflies, and crossed the A275 by the temporary lights. Just before Sheffield Park Bridge the path ducked through a hedge into a spreading meadow of thigh-high grasses. And there was the Ouse, all of a tumble, the sun skating off it in panes of light. It was a proper river now, passing between banks made impassable by a wild profusion of mugwort, nettles and Himalayan balsam. On the far side a dog rose had scrambled its way along the branches of an elder, and the little faded roses grew intertwined with flat creamy umbels that smelled precisely of June. The water was opaque and so full of sediment it looked liquid mud. Its surface caught and distorted the shadows of the plants and beneath them the castellated reflections of clouds slowly shuddered by.

I dropped down beneath an ash tree. My hair was wet at the nape, and my back was soaked with sweat. What a multitude of mirrors there are in the world! Each blade of grass seemed to catch the sun and toss it back to the sky. Big white clouds were pressing overhead and beneath them crossed electric blue damselflies, always in pairs and sometimes glued into a wincing knot. After a while, my brain cooled down. I sat up and drank some water and ate a slice of cheese. As I chewed, a movement at the field's edge caught my eye. A wave of golden air was working its way down the meadow, wheeling as it went. It moved like smoke, a persistent, particulate cloud made up of flakes of tumbled gold. Pollen. It was June; too late for alder and hazel, too late for willow. I weighed up the options: nettle or dock, plantain, oilseed or rape or – but it was less likely – pine. A pollen grain is identified by its architecture and ornamentation; it can be porous or furrowed, smooth or spiked. Plantain pollen is covered in verrucas; the pollen of golden rod bristles all over like a miniaturised pineapple. Echinate is the technical term for this latter design, meaning prickly, from *echinos*, the Greek for hedgehog.

Pollen is designed to drift. The tiny grains – hundreds of thousands in a single pinch – often have air sacs to help them float, as waterwings buoy a swimmer. These grains can travel great distances. In 2006 residents in East Anglia and Lincolnshire reported a pollen that covered cars and could be tasted on the air. It had come across the North Sea from Scandinavia and was seen on satellite pictures as a vast cloud: *a yellow-green plume sweeping the coast*, as the BBC report put it. Scientists identified it as birch pollen, the product of a wet April and sunny May in Denmark, though crop fires in western Russia may have contributed to the dust.

I leaned back and watched the cloud come. It could have crossed oceans, though it seemed more likely that it had risen from the neighbouring field, where coppery dock and nettle grew tangled amid the grasses. Didn't Plato think there was a wind that could impregnate horses? It couldn't have been more fertile than this generative swarm, twelve feet long and a yard wide, that rolled towards the waiting flowers.

Olivia Laing, To the River: A Journey Beneath the Surface, *2011*

Each season brings its magic, and summer's begins in the last week of June, as meadow flowers begin to weave a tapestry of subtle colour through fine meadow grasses.

In a local wildflower meadow, ox-eye daisies sway in the breeze. Their beautiful local name of 'moon daisy' describes them perfectly, for the yellow centre looks like the moon rising from its surrounding white petals. The name delights the children I tell this to, as I was delighted when my mother told me as a child. And it's not only children who enjoy the ox-eye daisies. I have watched fox cubs playing among them and occasionally pouncing on them as if they are prey.

Bird's-foot trefoil, known locally as Tom's Thumb, is also a delight with its bright, dainty yellow flowers and one thumb-like petal that inspired its name, the more so when a common blue settles on one of these fairytale flowers to sup nectar (an important primary food plant for this butterfly).

Threaded among these flowers are ribbons of yellow rattle, a semi-parasitic plant that feeds on the roots of meadow grasses, keeping them from densely covering the meadow so that wild-flowers can set seed. I love the soft flower heads of Yorkshire fog grass with their haze of pink here and there, and which, together with cocksfoot meadow grasses, are important larval food plants for a number of our butterfly larva.

A few days later among the grasses I find a field vole in a burrow and watch it scuttle across the burrow's entrance below ground. Then, walking quietly and softly along the path, I spot a basking grass snake, easily identified by its yellow collar, which is doubtless lying in wait for one of the many toads that inhabit this meadow. It slithers away as quickly and smoothly as ribbon across silk when it senses my presence.

A green woodpecker is feeding on ants on one of the ant-hills but it spots me and flies off with its 'yaffle' signal. As I am admiring it, my attention is caught by a kestrel ahead of me, hovering over and then diving onto an unsuspecting small mammal which it captures and carries away. Towards dusk, I have watched barn owls catching bank voles and field voles here, too, reminding me of the countless species that benefit from wild-flower meadows. A black, scimitar-winged bird flies swiftly past, scooping up insects low over the meadow. One of the glorious, uplifting sights of summer has passed within a whisker, and more swifts follow. I cannot imagine anything more beautiful or uplifting.

Greater and common knapweed are striking flowers that attract good numbers of marbled white butterflies, which will also sip nectar from the many florets of delicate field scabious. Meadow brown butterflies also vie to win the nectar of a particular flower.

The flowers also attract feisty Essex skipper butterflies who defend 'their' flowers from bumblebees. It's an impressive and determined stand from such a small butterfly towards a bumblebee. It's only female bumblebees that sting; can skipper butterflies tell the difference between male and female bees, I wonder?

Not far away an organic arable farm is impressively managed for wildlife and has a wildflower field margin. Here, there are at least four nesting pairs of skylarks, and as I arrive there in mid July, I hear their unmistakeable joyful summer song as they fly skywards. I kneel down to take a closer look at the small white flowers and delicate leaves of hedge bedstraw alongside a hedge. As I look, a shape moves from the crop into the grassy mown track which separates it from the field margin just a few feet away. It's a hare – so close that I can see its beautiful soft brown eyes, large ears with the distinctive black-topped tips and those large, powerful legs which allow it to run at speeds of up to forty-five miles an hour. It comes so close that I can no longer keep the camera in focus as I take photographs of it.

At home, an orchard meadow has replaced my lawn. It gives me constant surprises, such as finding, for the first time this year, a small copper butterfly on the wild marjoram there, and a beautiful wool carder bee on purple toadflax, which was sown by the wind from the flower border. Now that these essential native wildflowers and meadow grasses are all but lost in the countryside, our gardens can provide vital habitats. Unlike a lawn, my meadow only has to be mown from July or August onwards until December – three times at most. Surely, that alone must tempt you to transform part of your lawn into a wildflower or orchard meadow!

Jo Cartmell, 2016

Summer, June summer, with the green back on earth and the whole world unlocked and seething – like winter, it came suddenly and one knew it in bed, almost before waking up; with cuckoos and pigeons hollowing the word since daylight and the chipping of tits in the pear-blossom.

On the bedroom ceiling, seen first through sleep, was a pool of expanding sunlight – the lake's reflection thrown up through the trees by the rapidly climbing sun. Still drowsy, I watched on the ceiling above me its glittering image reversed, saw every motion of its somnambulant waves and projections of the life upon it. Arrows ran across it from time to time, followed by the far call of a moorhen; I saw ripples of light around each root of the bulrushes, every detail of the lake seemed there. Then suddenly the whole picture would break into pieces, would be smashed like a molten mirror and run amok in tiny globules of gold, frantic and shivering; and I would hear the great slapping of wings on water, building up a steady crescendo, while across the ceiling passed the shadows of swans taking off into the heavy morning. I would hear their cries pass over the house and watch the chaos of light above me, till it slowly settled and re-collected its stars and resumed the lake's still image.

Watching swans take off from my bedroom ceiling was a regular summer wakening. So I woke and looked out through the open window to a morning of cows and cockerels. The beech trees framing the lake and valley seemed to call for a

Royal Hunt; but they served equally well for climbing into, and even in June you could still eat their leaves, a tight-folded salad of juices.

Outdoors, one scarcely knew what had happened or re-membered any other time. There had never been rain, or frost, or cloud; it had always been like this. The heat from the ground climbed up one's legs and smote one under the chin. The gar-den, dizzy with scent and bees, burned all over with hot white flowers, each one so blinding an incandescence that it hurt the eyes to look at them.

The villagers took summer like a kind of punishment. The women never got used to it. Buckets of water were being sluiced down paths, the dust was being laid with grumbles, blankets and mattresses hung like tongues from the windows, panting dogs crouched under the rain-tubs. A man went by and asked 'Hot enough for 'ee?' and was answered by a worn-out shriek

In the builder's stable, well out of the sun, we helped to groom Brown's horse. We smelt the burning of his coat, the horn of his hooves, his hot leather harness, and dung. We fed him on bran, dry as a desert wind, till both we and the horse half-choked. Mr Brown and his family were going for a drive, so we wheeled the trap into the road, backed the blinkered horse between the shafts, and buckled his jingling straps. The road lay deserted in its layer of dust and not a thing seemed to move in the valley. Mr Brown and his best-dressed wife and daughter, followed by his bowler-hatted son-in-law, climbed one by one into the high sprung trap and sat there with ritual stiffness.

'Where are we goin' then, Father?'

'Up the hill, for some air.'

'Up the hill? He'll drop down dead.'

'Bide quiet,' said Mr Brown, already dripping with sweat, 'Another word, and you'll go back 'ome.'

He jerked the reins and gave a flick of the whip and the horse broke into a saunter. The women clutched their hats at the unexpected movement, and we watched them till they were out of sight.

When they were gone there was nothing else to look at, the village slipped back into silence. The untarred road wound away up the valley, innocent as yet of motor-cars, wound empty away to other villages, which lay empty too, the hot day long, waiting for the sight of a stranger.

We sat by the roadside and scooped the dust with our hand and made little piles in the gutters. Then we slid through the grass and lay on our backs and just stared at the empty sky. There was nothing to do. Nothing moved or happened, nothing happened at all except summer. Small heated winds blew over our faces, dandelion seeds floated by, burnt sap and roast nettles tingled our nostrils together with the dull rust smell of dry ground. The grass was June high and had come up with a rush, a massed entanglement of species, crested with flowers and spears of wild wheat, and coiled with clambering vetches, the whole of it humming with blundering bees and flickering with scarlet butterflies. Chewing grass on our backs, the grass scaffolding the sky, the summer was all we heard; the cuckoos crossed distances of chains of cries, flies buzzed and choked in the ears, and the saw-toothed chatter of mowing-machines drifted waves of fair from the fields.

We moved. We went to the shop and bought sherbet and sucked it through sticks of liquorice. Sucked gently, the sherbet merely dusted the tongue; too hard, and you choked with sweet powders; or if you blew back through the tube the sherbet-bag burst and you disappeared in a blizzard of sugar. Sucking and blowing, coughing and weeping, we scuffled our way down the lane. We drank at the spring to clean our mouths, then threw water at each other and made rainbows. Mr Jones's pond was bubbling with life, and covered with great white lilies – they poured from their leaves like candle-fat, ran molten, then cooled on the water. Moorhens plopped, and dabchicks scooted, insects rowed and skated. New-hatched frogs hopped about like flies, lizards gulped in the grass. The lane itself was crusted with cow-dung, hard baked and smelling good.

We met Sixpence Robinson among the bulrushes, and he said, 'Come and have some fun.' He lived along the lane just past the sheepwash in a farm cottage near a bog. There were five in his family, two girls and three boys, and their names all began with S. There was Sis and Sloppy, Stosher and Sammy, and our good friend Sixpence the Tanner. Sis and Sloppy were both beautiful girls and used to hide from us boys in the gooseberries. It was the brothers we played with: and Sammy, though a cripple, was one of the most agile lads in the village.

Theirs was a good place to be at any time, and they were good to be with. (Like us, they had no father; unlike ours, he was dead.) So today, in the spicy heat of their bog, we sat round on logs and whistled, peeled sticks, played mouth-organs, dammed up the stream, and cut harbours in the cool clay banks. Then we took all the pigeons out of their dovecots and ducked them in the water-butt, held them under till their beaks started bubbling them threw them up in the air. Splashing spray from their wings they flew round the house, then came back to roost like fools. (Sixpence had a one-eyed pigeon called Spike who he boasted could stay under longest, but one day the poor bird, having broken all records, crashed for ever among the cabbages.)

When all this was over, we retired to the paddock and played cricket under the trees. Sammy, in his leg-irons, charged up and down. Hens and guinea-fowl took to the trees. Sammy hopped and bowled like murder at us, and we defended our stumps with our lives. The cracked bat clouting; the cries in the reeds; the smells of fowls and water; the long afternoon with the steep hills around us watched by Sloppy still hid in the gooseberries – it seemed down here that no disasters could happen, that nothing could ever touch us. This was Sammy's and Sixpence's; the place past sheepwash, the hide-out unspoiled by authority, where drowned pigeons flew and cripples ran free; where it was summer, in some ways, always.

Summer was also the time of these: of sudden plenty, of slow hours and actions, of diamond haze and dust on the eyes, of the valley in post-vernal slumber; of burying birds out of seething corruption; of Mother sleeping heavily at noon; of jazzing wasps and dragonflies, haystooks and thistle-seeds, snows of white butterflies, skylarks' eggs, bee-orchids, and frantic ants; of wolf-cub parades, and boy scouts' bugles; of sweat running down the legs; of boiling potatoes on bramble fires, of flames glass-blue in the sun; of lying naked in the hill-cold stream; begging pennies for bottles of pop; of girls' bare arms and unripe cherries, green apples and liquid walnuts; of fights and falls and new-scabbed knees, sobbing pursuits and flights; of picnics high up in the crumbling quarries, of butter running like oil, of sunstroke, fever, and cucumber peel stuck cool to one's burning brow. All this, and the feeling that it would never end, that such days had come for ever, with the pump drying up and the water-butt crawling, and the chalk ground hard as the moon. All sights twice-brilliant and smell twice-sharp, all game-days twice as long. Double charged as we were, like the meadow ants, with the frenzy of the sun, we used up the light to its last violet drop, and even then couldn't go to bed.

When darkness fell, and the huge moon rose, we stirred to a second life. Then boys went calling along the roads, wild slit-eyed animal calls, Walt Kerry's naked nasal yodel, Boney's jackal scream. As soon as we heard them we crept outdoors, out of our stifling bedrooms, stepped out into moonlight warm as the sun to join our chalk-white, moon-masked gang.

Games in the moon. Games of pursuit and capture. Games that the night demanded. Best of all, Fox and Hounds – go where you like, and the whole of the valley to hunt through. Two chosen boys loped away through the trees and were immediately swallowed in the shadow. We gave them five minutes, then set off after them. They had churchyard, farmyard, barns, quarries, hilltops, and woods to run to. They had all night, and the whole of the moon, and five miles of country to hide in. . . .

Padding softly, we ran under the melting stars, through sharp garlic woods, through blue blazed fields, following the scent by the game's one rule, the question and answer cry. Every so often, panting for breath, we paused to check on our quarry. Bullet heads lifted, teeth shone in the moon. 'Whistle-or-'OLLER! Or-we-shall-not-FOLLER!' It was a cry on two notes, prolonged. From the other side of the hill, above white fields on mist, the faint fox-cry came back. We were off again then, through the waking night, among sleepless owls and badgers, while our quarry slipped off into another parish and would not be found for hours.

Round about midnight we ran them to earth, exhausted under a haystack. Until then we had chased them all through the world, through jungles, swamps, and tundras, across pampas plains and steppes of wheat and plateaux of shooting starts, while hares made love in the silver grasses, and the hot large moon climbed over us, raising tides in my head of night and summer that move there even yet.

Laurie Lee, Cider with Rosie, *1959*

I leave the sleepy village of half a dozen houses and head off over the stile, following a small path which rises steeply through lush grass and fresh bracken stems. It's muddy and in damper conditions would be ankle deep and slippery, but today it's baked dry, pitted with the hooves of livestock. A thin layer of high cloud softens the fierceness of the Scottish sun, and skylarks pour out their song as they hang in the air, then flutter to earth.

The sea has just come into view, shimmering, blue, calm, expansive. I pause for breath and pick up the perfume of gorse, marvelling at the vibrant yellow flowers packed so tightly between the prickles.

I climb up the cliff, following the path which soon levels out, leaving the gorse bushes behind. I am surrounded by flowers and serenaded with birdsong. The path meanders up and down the folds in the landscape, and with the sea on my right I look for a place to rest. Most of the ground is too steep and stony for comfort, but eventually my search is rewarded. Moving a protruding briar and a couple of stones I get out the thermos. Butterflies flit from flower to flower, while a nearby rock pipit furiously protests that I have invaded his patch.

From this point there is a wide arc of deep blue sparkling sea visible, the horizon hidden in heat haze. About thirty metres below me I can see a stretch of beach and hear the waves lapping the rocks. A pair of oystercatchers fly past, skimming the water and scolding loudly, their bright red beaks and black and white plumage glinting in the sun. Some terns arrive, screeching with excitement as they dive into the sea, then fly up again before the water droplets have settled.

My eye is caught by a flash of white out to sea. A gannet! I watch as it flies in great arcs across the sea and then suddenly swoops, folding its great wings at the last moment. It enters the sea like an arrow and I'm sure I can hear the impact. I use binoculars to watch the area where it disappeared, and in a few minutes it bobs up like a cork, fish in beak. It has to heave on its wings in order to become airborne, only to repeat the process time and time again. I could watch it for hours. Eventually it flies off, close to the water, crop heavy with fish.

The tide must be at its lowest point by now and as the waves rise and fall in the bay below me, rocks and seaweed appear and disappear in the swell. Then three dark shapes appear about a metre or so out to sea. First they're there, then they're gone. It's definitely not rocks or seaweed. What is it? A seal? It's too small and seals don't normally behave like that. I watch, fascinated, and train the binoculars on it. This time when it dives, I see a tail quite clearly. It must be an otter! He makes his way along the bay – always a metre or two from the shore line. He dives and resurfaces, takes a look round then dives again, both playful and industrious at the same time. Eventually he moves behind a large rock out of my line of vision. The clouds thin and I consider closing my eyes and nodding off in the warmth when I see the three dark shapes again, head, body and tail. A moment ago they were to the left of that dark patch of sea. Then *in* the dark patch and now to the right of it. He's making his way, slowly but surely, towards me.

When he finally arrives directly in front of me, he turns and heads towards the beach. I watch him come ashore not twenty metres away. His wet fur glistens in the sun and his sleek, lithe body appears to flow over and around the rocks. There's something in his mouth. He finally comes to rest on a large flat rock and holds the fish in his front paws. The water drops on his long snout whiskers shine and sparkle as he proceeds to chew off a mouthful. He spills morsels on the ground and chews with his mouth open, which lets me see his sharp, pointed, white teeth. The fish looks tough for he moves his head and jaw up and down in an effort to pull it to pieces.

He seems completely at home in his environment, quite unselfconscious, oblivious of my presence, totally involved in the business of eating and living his life as he does every day. I feel as though I'm spying on him, intruding into his private world. Does the fact that I consider it a privilege to witness such behaviour make it any less intrusive? I don't know. What I do know is that in these special brief moments, I feel as if we are locked in a secret liaison. I am totally focused on this fascinating, elusive wild creature. In this brief time I am, like him, living and breathing in a moment that appears to last for ever.

Now he's back to the water for a second course. The next two catches are of smaller creatures – I can't tell what they are – perhaps crabs. He's brought them both back to the same rock before eating them. The incoming tide soon engulfs the rock and the otter makes his way further along the shore. He moves out of sight, but not out of mind. He is the first otter I've ever seen, and I'm thrilled.

Janet Willoner, 2016

Overlooking the River Stour

The swallows flew in the curves of an eight
Above the river-gleam
In the wet June's last beam:
Like little crossbows animate
The swallows flew in the curves of an eight
Above the river-gleam.

Planing up shavings of crystal spray
A moor-hen darted out
From the bank thereabout,
And through the stream-shine ripped his way;
Planing up shavings of crystal spray
A moor-hen darted out.

Closed were the kingcups; and the mead
Dripped in monotonous green,
Though the day's morning sheen
Had shown it golden and honeybee'd;
Closed were the kingcups; and the mead
Dripped in monotonous green.

And never I turned my head, alack,
While these things met my gaze
Through the pane's drop-drenched glaze,

To see the more behind my back . . .
O never I turned, but let, alack,
These less things hold my gaze!

Thomas Hardy, published 1917

B lack and shadowy are not words usually connected with summer, a season generally considered to be one of colour and warmth, brightening our moods with pastel-shaded landscapes of foxglove and poppy. But against this backdrop another world exists, less colourful and obvious, although just as vibrant, for summer's tapestry is interwoven with a wide variety of shades. Many creatures – the black, the drab and the furtive – hide from the sun and daylight in the damper, shadier areas of our gardens and homes, those pockets of darkness among summery tints.

As the sun sinks in a blaze of orange and copper streaks, daylight begins to fade. The summer triangle of stars appears in turquoise skies, and the first bats start to emerge, before other nocturnal mammals like foxes and hedgehogs.

The old-fashioned name for a bat is 'flittermouse', a nickname that suits them very well, as they flicker above the garden in the dusk air. Bats' furry skin ranges in colour from pale brown to black, and they spend daytime hours roosting in the shadows of houses, crevices and trees. They fly on webbed, fingery-boned wings using echolocation to source their prey. Their staple diet is small flying insects such as midges, gnats and moths, and despite their diminutive size each bat can eat up to three thousand insects a night. It is a pleasure to watch bats swoop and dance in the roseate glow of the sleepy sun, while bees still hum among the herb and thistle beds, before becoming dark fleeting shadows against the backdrop of an amber hay moon.

When gazing up at bats, it appears to be a soundless world. Pipistrelles are the species most likely to be spotted above our gardens. In the 1990s they were separated into two distinct species, common and soprano, the distinguishing feature being their high frequency calls, a noise inaudible to human ears. Using a bat detector brings the sounds of the bat world alive. They are not silent at all but emit an assortment of chirrups, clicks and warbles.

Detectors are also able to identify when a bat captures prey, and devours its victim with a gratifying slurp. While they feed in the dewy softness of dusk and the evening chorus of birdsong fills the air with bells and harps, one of the most turbulent and powerful battles in the natural world is underway, the everevolving abattoir known as the food chain.

Many animals, birds and bats eat insects. Even insects eat insects. This poses a conundrum for nature lovers, especially entomologists. On creating a bug-friendly garden, there is a hint of irony to see a wren hopping on top of the log pile, with a beak full of transparent wings and spindly legs, or to hear the whack of a snail's shell as it is hammered against a song thrush's anvil. Even in the height of enchanted summer hours, there is no room for sentimentality when it comes to nature's menu.

Like bats, many insects are dark coloured and live in the damp, shaded parts of our gardens, under stones, slate, tree bark, logs, rotting wood, leaf litter, compost, shells, plant pots; in fact insects will use anything as long as the conditions are right. If we look closely at the dingy, cooler places, we find a world worth exploring and just as wonderful as the discoveries in a seashore rock pool. It may not be high on everyone's 'to do' summer list, but there is nothing nicer than crawling along the ground, feeling the soggy dampness of grass on your knees, and the squelchy, slippery sensation of mud squeezing through your fingers. Entering the world of ground-dwelling bugs is a bit like stepping into an old church on a stifling summer's afternoon where inside it is cool, musty and dim. It feels like another world, although outside the sun still shines, birds carry on singing and the sky remains blue.

The dank world of insects and bugs is enlivened by an array of scents, textures and colours. Damp wood is often lightened by splashes of verdant moss and lime-green lichen. These moist environments smell earthy and woody, and are just as invigorating as the perfumed fragrances of rose and honeysuckle. There are many things to touch: the steely hardness of stone, the rough, corrugated grooves of bark and even the delicate tickle of the creatures themselves.

It is a wonderful experience to come across hidden clusters of flaxen pearls among leaf litter. These are slug eggs, glittering like jewels among the leafy carpets of brown and gold. One of the most common and fascinating creatures are woodlice; when disturbed they scurry frantically, looking like a troop of armoured tanks surprised in battle. From a distance they look grey and uninteresting, but through a magnifying glass it is sometimes possible to catch hints of mottled pink, yellow or white against the silvery sheen of evening dew.

When dusk fades, nature's handover takes place. Creatures of the night pick up the baton. With colouring that complements the darker tones of night, bats twirl in starlight and small, daytime-shy bugs sneak from their hiding places as nasturtium heads nod in sleep. Within each seasonal hue, every creature has its place, and even in summertime the dark, shady places are teeming with life.

Jacqueline Bain, 2016

The richest, fullest time of year is when June is wearing to an end, when one knows without the almanac that spring is over and gone. Nowhere in England is one more sensible of the change to fullest summer than in this low-lying, warmest corner of Hampshire.

The cuckoo ceases to weary us with its incessant call, and the nightingale sings less and less frequently. The passionate season is well-nigh over for the birds; their fountain of music begins to run dry. The cornfields and waste grounds are everywhere splashed with the intense scarlet of poppies. Summer has no rain in all her wide, hot heavens to give to her thirsty fields and has sprinkled them with the red fiery moisture from her own veins. And as colour changes, growing deeper and more intense, so do sounds change: for the songs of yesterday there are shrill hunger-cries.

One of the oftenest heard in all the open woods, in hedges, and even out in the cornfields is the curious musical call of the young blackbird. It is like the chuckle of the adult, but not so loud, full, happy, and prolonged; it is shriller, and drops at the end to a plaintive, impatient sound, a little pathetic – a cry of the young bird to its too long absent mother. When very hungry he emits this shrill musical call at intervals of ten to fifteen seconds; it may be heard distinctly a couple of hundred yards away.

The numbers of young blackbirds and throstles apparently just out of the nest astonish one. They are not only in the copses and hedges, and on almost every roadside tree, but you constantly see them on the ground in the lanes and public roads, standing still, quite unconscious of danger. The poor helpless bird looks up at you in a sort of amazement, never having seen men walking or riding on bicycles; but he hesitates, not knowing whether to fly away or stand still. Thrush or blackbird, he is curiously interesting to look at. The young thrush, with his yellowish-white spotty breast, the remains of down on his plumage his wide yellow mouth, and raised head with large, fixed, toad-like eyes, has a distinctly reptilian appearance. Not so the young blackbird standing motionless on the road, in doubt too as to what you are; his short tail raised giving him an incipient air of blackbird jauntiness; his plumage not brown, indeed, as we describe it, but rich chestnut black, like the chestnut-black hair of a beautiful Hampshire girl of that precious type with oval face and pale dark skin. A pretty creature, rich in colour, with a musical pathetic voice, waiting so patiently to be visited and fed, and a weasel perhaps watching him from the roadside grass with hungry, bright little eyes! How they die – thrushes and blackbirds – at this perilous period in their lives! I sometimes see what looks like a rudely-painted figure of a bird on the hard road: it is a young blackbird that had not the sense to get out of the way of a passing team, and was crushed flat by a hoof or wheel. It is but one in a thousand that perishes in that way. One has to remember that these two species of thrush-throstle and blackbird – are in extraordinary abundance, that next to starlings and chaffinches they abound over all species; that they are exceedingly prolific, beginning to lay in this southern county in February, and rearing at least three broods in the season; and that when winter comes round again the thrush and blackbird population will be just about what it was before.

Fruit-eating birds to not much vex the farmer in this almost fruitless country. Thrushes and finches and sparrows are nothing to him: the starling, if he pays any attention to the birds, he looks on us as a good friend.

At the farm there are two very old yew trees growing in the back-yard, and one of these, in an advanced state of decay, is full of holds and cavities in its larger branches. Here about half-a-dozen pairs of starlings nest every year, and by the middle of June there are several broods of fully-fledged young. At this time it was amusing to watch the parent birds at their task, coming and going all day long, flying out and away straight as arrows to this side and that, every bird to its own favourite hunting-ground. Some had their grounds in the meadow, just before the house where the cows and geese were, and it was easy to watch their movements. Out of the yew the bird would shoot, and in ten or twelve seconds would be down walking about in that busy, plodding, rook-like way the starling has when looking for something; and presently, darting his beak into the turf, he would drag out something large, and back he would fly to his young with a big, conspicuous, white object in his beak. These white objects which he was busily gathering every day, from dawn to dark, were full-grown grubs of the cockchafer. When watching these birds at their work it struck me that the enormous increase of starlings all over the country in recent years may account for the fact that great cockchafer years do not now occur. In former years these beetles were sometimes in such numbers that they swarmed in the air in places, and stripped the oaks of their leaves in mid-summer. It is now more than ten years since I saw cockchafers in considerable numbers, and for a long time past I have not heard of their appearance in swarms anywhere.

The starling is in some ways a bad bird, a cherry thief, and a robber of other birds' nesting-places; yaffle and nuthatch must hate him, but if his ministrations have caused an increase of even one per cent, in the hay crop, and the milk and butter supply, he is, from our point of view, not wholly bad.

In late June the unkept hedges are in the fullness of their midsummer beauty. After sunset the fragrance of the honeysuckle is almost too much: standing near the blossom-laden hedge when there is no wind to dissipate the odour, there is a heaviness in it which makes it like some delicious honeyed liquor which we are drinking in. The honeysuckle is indeed first among the 'melancholy flowers' that give out their fragrance by night. In the daytime, when the smell is faint, the pale sickly blossoms are hardly noticed even where they are seen in masses and drape the hedges. Of all the hedge-flowers, the rose alone is looked at, its glory being so great as to make all other blooms seem nothing but bleached or dead discoloured leaves in comparison.

He would indeed be a vainly ambitious person who should attempt to describe this queen of all wild flowers, joyous or melancholy; but substituting flower for fruit, and the delight of the eye for the pleasure of taste, we may in speaking of it quote the words of a famous old writer, used in praise of the strawberry. He said that doubtless God Almighty could have made a better berry if He had so minded, but doubtless God Almighty never did.

I esteem the rose not only for that beauty which sets it highest among flowers, but also because it will not suffer admiration when removed from its natural surroundings. In this particular it resembles certain brilliant sentient beings that languish and lose all their charms in captivity. Pluck your rose and bring it indoors, and place it side by side with other blossoms – yellow flag and blue periwinkle, and shining yellow marsh-marigold, and poppy and cornflower – and it has no luster, and is no more to the soul than a flower made out of wax or paper. Look at it here, in the brilliant sunlight and the hot wind, waving to the wind on its long thorny sprays all over the vast disordered hedges; here in rosy masses, there starring the rough green tangle with its rosy stars – a rose-coloured cloud on the earth and Summer bridal veil – and you will refuse to believe (since it will be beyond your power to imagine) that anywhere on earth, in any hot or temperate climate, there exist a more divinely beautiful sight.

W. H. Hudson, Hampshire Days, *1903*

On a summer night I look up, absorbing the darkness. It takes a few seconds for my eyes to adjust, to focus on the incandescent balls of gas that decorate the sky. Its magnitude is breathtaking: endless possibilities in all directions, clusters of magic in gentle shades of blue, white, pink and orange. I'm no expert at stargazing, but I lose myself simply looking.

The Plough is the first constellation to reveal itself. Part of the Ursa Major, the Great Bear, it never sinks below the horizon. As a result it remains by my side all year round, a familiar friend in the sky. In the summer months it rests higher up, the bowl of its saucepan shape leaning towards the ground as if beckoning us to touch it. Using the right-hand stars of the Plough as a guide I locate Polaris, the North Star. I find it comforting that this star, 434 light years away, offers humans a safe navigational tool to locate true north.

Stars march across the sky in all directions, exploding balls of hydrogen and helium illuminating the night sky. I am seeking out my favourite constellation, Orion, a Greek hunter trapped among the stars. The easiest starting point is his belt, and before you know it, his shoulders and feet appear. He commands the sky, his shoulders stretching broadly, his feet sturdy and secure. A dark night like tonight also reveals the Orion nebula, a fuzzy patch that simmers at the tip of his sword. Using my telescope, I can make out a beautiful swirling pattern of dust. Moving within it are oxygen, silicon and other minerals which make up many of the rocks here on Earth. This tiny patch of dust, no bigger than a dot in the dark sky, is 1,600 light years away and yet 167 million million miles wide. I am in awe.

Like everything on Earth, space is not exempt from death. A supernova – the death of a star – explodes through space. The death is quick, taking only a few seconds, yet it is transformed into something sublime and radiant. As it releases more energy, the star's brightness increases a hundred million times. All of its elements are thrown back into the galaxy, becoming part of the interstellar gas and dust that forms the next generation of stars. Life begins again. Without the death of a star, planets would not exist, including Earth. We have stars to thank for the unique blue and green planet we call home.

I think of the cities too brightly polluted for the stars to be visible, and feel great loss on behalf of both stars and city. For the gaze of the moon staring down at you, and its surrounding family of stars, is a spectacle under which many children grow up without ever really seeing it. Give the gift of the stars. Whenever you can, encourage the young to look up and immerse themselves into the greater universe we're part of. Taking notice of the galaxy is good for us. It awakens our souls.

Emma Oldham, 2016

July

July 1. Full moon. Cherries begin to ripen, but are devoured by sparrows. Began to cut my meadow-hay, a good crop, one 3rd more than last year.

July 2. The early brood of swallows are active & adroit, & able to procure their subsistence on the wing. Fresh broods come forth daily.

July 3. Black-caps are great thieves among the cherries. The flycatcher is a very harmless & honest bird, medling with nothing but insects.

July 5. Field-crickets are pretty near silent; they begin their shrilling cry about the middle of May.

July 6. The bees that have not swarmed lie clustering round the mouths of the hives. Took-off the frames from the cucum^{rs}: those under the hand-glasses begin to show fruit. Hay lies in a bad state.

July 8. Second swarm of bees on the same bough of the balm of Gilead fir. Turned the hay-cocks which are in a bad state. Cherries delicate, Mr Grimm, my artist, came from London to take some of our finest views.

July 9. The bees are very quarrelsome, & stung me.

July 10. Some of the little frogs from the ponds stroll quite up the hill: they seem to spread in all directions.

July 11. *Tilia europaea.* The lime blows, smells very sweetly,

& affords much pabulum for bees. *Footnote.* Bees come & suck the cherries where the birds have broke the skin; & on some autumns, I remember they attack'd & devoured the peaches & Nect: where the wasps had once made a beginning.

July 14. Young frogs migrate, & spread around the ponds for more than a furlong: they march about all day long, separating in pursuit of food; & get to the top of the hill, & into the N. field.

July 16. Bees, when a shower approaches, hurry home. One hive of bees does not swarm; the bees lie in clusters at the mouth of the hive.

July 19. *Sambucus ebulus.* Dwarf elder [Dane's elder] blows. Fungi begin to appear.

July 21. Missle thrushes bring forth their broods, & flock together.

July 22. Bees swarm: the swarm of a swarm, which swarmed itself at the beginning of June. A neighbor has had nine swarms from four stalls [mother-hives]: two apiece from three of them, & three from one.

July 23. Walnuts abound, but are rather small & spotted.

July 25. Bees that have not swarmed kill their drones.

July 26. Cut the grass in the little meadow. Hay makes well. Hops fill their poles, & throw out lateral shoots.

July 30. Peacocks begin to moult & cast their splendid train. Total eclipse of the moon.

Reverend Gilbert White, The Naturalist's Journal, *1776*

The colour of July is gold. Gold now are the barley fields which cover much of Norfolk. Gold in the sheltered eyes of hares, the clambering harvest mice, the gapes of skylark chicks against the dirt. Gold the corn marigold blooms at the field's edge, where spared the spray, gold on the backs of probing hoverflies.

Gold, too, are the grasses in uncut meadows and verges. Not yet the sad dun of wind-torn winter but gold already with autumn, their breeding, seeding done, as the balance of the year tips – so soon? – towards shorter nights and colder. Gold in the happy ragwort flowers here, gold in the fleabane where the water sits, gold in the burnished eyes of grasshoppers singing for summer never to cease.

By our coast there is gold in the bills of little terns, fidgeting like finger puppets over the beach, bringing silvered sand-eels to their sand-hunkered chicks. Nearby on a scrape stand yellow-legged gulls, loafing here on a summer break from the continent, their legs eponymous. Gold, among the stubbornly green reed in the fen, the flowers of yellow loosestrife and greater bird's-foot trefoil. Gold the long-horn beetle's wing-shields, blotched and spotted with black. *Strangalia maculata*, the evocative name of this bejewelled brooch of a bug.

There is gold in people's faces too, as they enjoy the smells, the sounds, the sights of summer, small and big. The sun has turned their arms and the backs of their necks gold, and the legs of shorts-clad children splodging through a saltmarsh past the rayless gold flowers of sea aster.

It is here that the true treasure lies, the crock of gold: in the relationship that holidays allow our children to build with nature, the horizon-stretching freedom of the summer. Now can children build dams in streams; make shelters in the woods; crawl through bracken on their tummies; crush and smell wild garlic or sea wormwood leaves; and be free.

Nick Acheson, 2016

Yellow Iris

It's early morning
and a woman
from a previous
world is wading
up the stream.

Very stately and
sturdy with double-
jointed elbows she's
still in her
grave clothes,
her crinkled three-ply
surcoat made of
cloth of June.

She has one
gold-webbed glove,
one withered hand.

She's resting, considering
her next pose,
behind the blades
of slatted blinds.

Her name is
Iris, the Rainbow,
the messenger, the
water's secretary, the
only word she
speaks is 'yellow'.

Lost ghost Queen
of the Unbetween
it's lovely listening
to the burp
of mud as
she sinks her
feet right in.

Alice Oswald, 2009

The glass orbs caught the sun and sparkled like jewels on the seashore. At first glance, it seemed as if a shipment of clear jack marbles had capsized, casting its precious cargo into the waves. Some lay on the sand, immobile and perfect, others tumbled back into the surf, glinting and gleaming as they rolled.

The children were instantly drawn to the diamond treasure, like pirates. 'Don't touch them!' I cried, for surely these strange creatures were baby jellyfish, just waiting to sting inquisitive fingers or careless toes. There were hundreds, probably thousands along the shoreline; it was hard to avoid standing on them.

I looked more closely. Each was a perfect sphere of transparent, gelatinous life. Down its sides were delicately etched serrated lines and, in the centre, was that a mouth and a network of nerves? I concluded they had no apparent way of stinging. Like the children, I was itching to touch them, so we each oh so gently picked one up. They sparkled on the palms of our hands and, reassuringly, there was no jellyfish zap of pain.

My daughter's wonder quickly gave way to concern because so many of these little creatures were becoming stranded as the tide went out. The hot July sun was intense on our skin, making the sand warm to stand on. It meant that some of these little beings had lost their plump shape to become sad, squished blobs, glittering no more. 'We must save them,' she declared.

With the intense industry that only children can show, they began throwing the stranded orbs out to sea. I joined them in their labour, but with the adult's knowledge that it was an impossible task; for every one that glinted through the air to plop into the water, a hundred were washed back in. In the sea, about five metres out, a grey seal raised its head above the waterline, appraising us curiously before disappearing out of sight. Only the lure of ice creams could pull the children away from their vigil.

Back home, my son, ever keen to get his hands on the iPad, suggested we find out what they were. The answer was not baby jellyfish; in fact they are totally unrelated to jellyfish. They are instead little animals sometimes known as a comb jelly or more formally, ctenophore. They are also known as sea gooseberries. That name was perfect; they did indeed look exactly like gooseberries that had been laser sculpted from glass.

In the water, these little animals move themselves along by pulsating their serrated lines of tiny hairs, called cilia, which I had noticed. When the sea gooseberry beats its cilia, it sends iridescent shimmers along its body. Despite seeming so vulnerable and delicate on the beach that day, they are also voracious predators. They extend tentacles out from inside their bodies to catch tiny worms, fish eggs, larvae and even other sea gooseberries.

On our trip to the beach we had expected the usual sand in the sandwiches and ice cream bribe for good behaviour. We had made sandcastles and jumped off the dunes. But then nature surprised us and reminded us of all the hidden mysteries of the sea. When you reach out your hand and risk being stung, you start to care passionately about the creatures we share our world with.

Kate Blincoe, 2016

I f a psycho-analyst ever worked me over with a word-association test and threw out 'summer' for a starter, he would get an entire scenario in response.

It is a sultry afternoon. No sun. There are big castles of alto-cumulus which press the heat down. Elms bulge with foliage over a broad lawn. Unstirred by the faintest breeze, the leaves are draped heavy-layered as blankets on a bed in winter.

A faded rope hammock is slung between two apple trees. I've been mucking about in it, trying to spin it round like a chair-o-plane. Now I'm sprawled half asleep, gazing up through seaweedy greenness, thick and suffocating, to patches of light. The sky has become a pewter lid clamped heavily over the soupy stillness.

Part of the stillness is the drone of insects, a dynamo hum, but nearest is the sawing rasp of grasshoppers in the awns where bryony scrambles out from the untidy garden hedge. There is also a thin grating call – attached to the only movement in the dream-like languor. Repeatedly a sparrow-sized bird with streaked pale breast darts out, whirligigs up to snatch a winged ant, and swoops back to its launching-pad twig.

The scene is fixed in childhood, at an aunt's house. Is it a mosaic of different visits? Did one moment etch itself in my mind forever as the very photogravure of mid-summer?

I can't tell. But that bird – a spotted flycatcher, I later knew – became for me an essential presence in the year's high noon when gardens are overblown and stupefied with scents. Amid the torpor the flycatcher is a sprite, mousily plumaged yet whose vivacity puts a pulse of electricity through the air.

Last autumn, I knocked together a nesting box with a shelf-shaped bowl and nailed it to the lime whose boughs fan across the grass to the mill stream. Flycatchers like a lookout on the edge of a clear hunting space. I hoped my ready-made flat might persuade a pair to spend the summer with me.

By the middle of May none had turned up, and I forgot about it. This week through a window my eye was caught by an antic twirl of fawn wings. As if it was that moment of forty years ago returned, I watched the flycatcher corkscrew and flicker down upon a cabbage white butterfly and heard that finger-nail-scratching-glass call.

With its catch pincered in its bill, it swished over to the lime: a little spasm of bright energy against the green lassitude where a woodpigeon was groaning with boredom.

Since then two flycatchers are hunting over the lawn, all through the day up to the long twilight, spry air aces who seem never to muff an attack. Once that brilliant eye has fixed on a passing crane-fly, dodge though it might that crane-fly is (you might say) a dead duck.

They are now building a nest: a furious freighting of shreds of lichen snatched from the pear trees, cobwebs plucked from under the loggia supported by the huge oak pillar which was once the axis of the dismantled mill wheel, and (what spondulicks!) combings from the dogs' coats which had snarled up on the rose bushes.

Where did mine come from on those fast but frail wings? Natal, possibly, or even Asia, and it will be a brief stay.

By September's end they, and their young, will have flown south on their ten thousand mile odyssey – such an outlay to make an English summer complete.

Kenneth Allsop, In the Country, *1973*

Early July: the woodland was exquisite, glowing with shimmering green light and vividly animated with butterflies, ringlets and large skippers nectaring on the bramble flowers, but I barely noticed it, my heartbeat already accelerating, picking up speed with every step towards . . . the treasure. It was a hot bright morning and I began to perspire as we slogged up the path through the trees, four of us in single file with me, the initiate, bringing up the rear: the other three had seen the treasure before. Were their senses quivering with anticipation like mine? You know what? I think they probably were.

They turned off the path then, suddenly, at some barely perceptible marker I never saw, and dived into the trackless undergrowth and I followed, stumbling across the slope and clambering over fallen trunks until eventually, deep in the woods, we came to a small fenced enclosure; and there inside it, in the dappled shade of a young beech tree, was the end of the quest: three slender stems each bearing half a dozen purplish-pink blossoms. I gazed on them, spellbound.

Why do orchids excite us so? What is it about them that triggers, in those who begin to feel the passion for them, passion which is so extraordinary, passion which can lead not just to enchantment and delight but to covetousness, cupidity and criminal greed? I have spent a long time thinking about this and I have gradually come to believe it is because orchids are the flagbearers, the standard-bearers for one of the great revolutions in life on earth: the emergence of the flowering plants. What a remarkable revolution it was: 500 million years ago, the first plants that began to cover the land surface, which were pollinated by the wind, bore only one colour, that of their chlorophyll, green; yet about 150 million years ago, some of them began to employ insects instead of the breeze to move their pollen around, and equipped their reproductive organs with brightly-coloured petals to catch the insects' eyes, and so, in a great outburst of beauty, flowers were born. A flower to us may be loveliness made manifest, but we should not forget that in evolutionary terms it is merely a device to attract a pollinator; and since orchids are the largest plant family, with more than 25,000 species in the wild, they have had to compete fiercely amongst themselves to devise ever more eye-catching forms and colours to entice their insect helpers, in the dim light of the rainforest, where most of them evolved.

The result: these are the most glamorous, exotic, outlandish, beautiful blooms on earth, in the tropics, especially. I go to look at them in the glasshouses of Kew Gardens, this great cream six-pointed star from Madagascar, this pale purple bell with a yellow-orange heart from the Colombian Andes, this bizarre maroon-spotted cross from Borneo, and I see at once, these are flowers taken to the limit, they are the very epitome of florality, they are flowers set apart: they are the priestly caste of the plant kingdom.

Britain's orchids, with one great exception, are not riotously exotic in their beauty like their tropical cousins, yet I love them most of all, for their loveliness which is restrained: they are blooms of the temperate world, elegant spikes of tiny flowers in pastel shades, pink, cream, pale violet, pale purple, which sometimes seem to me in their understatement to be very English: plants designed by a civil servant. But they are nonetheless touched with distinction: they too are members of the priestly caste. In the meadow or on the downs or in the woodland, they stand out. We have just over fifty species and every year, like many others, I go looking for them, burnt orchid, spotted orchid, fragrant orchid, marsh orchid, pyramidal orchid, man orchid, lady orchid, bee orchid, and my favourite, greater butterfly orchid, an enchanting slender tower of separate, small creamy blooms you find trembling in the shade. Excitement attaches to encountering every one. In their beauty they are among the great signifiers of summer, like the woodland butterfly trio of white admiral, silver-washed fritillary and purple emperor, or that other trio in the sky, the 'summer triangle' of the stars Altair, Deneb and Vega.

Yet it is not just beauty which provides the allure: there is rarity too, the attraction of which seems to be hard-wired in our genes. Orchids are not just the largest plant family on earth, they are the most threatened, as a direct result of unrestrained human desire for them, and many have been driven by collectors to extinction in the wild; in Britain, several of our species, such as the military orchid, are among our least common flowers, and three head the list of our supreme rarities: the ghost orchid, the lady's slipper and the red helleborine. The first I suppose I may never see, as it is a mysterious small pale flower which only intermittently appears, deep in the leaf litter of the woodlands: it was last seen in 2009, and before that, in 1986. The second is a celebrity: the lady's slipper is the one British orchid which in its appearance unmistakably belongs with its tropical cousins. The flower's lip, or central lower petal, is huge, blousy and bright banana-yellow, shaped like a shoe or a slipper or a clog – a piece of footwear, certainly – while behind, the other petals that frame it are drooping pennants of intense maroon. It is gaudy, glitzy and totally over the top, it is unique in the British flora, and not just for its looks, but for its story. For the British population of the lady's slipper was driven by collectors to extinction's very edge: it was reduced to one single plant, guarded in total secrecy by a small group of devoted botanists for more than sixty years, until eventually, in the 1990s, scientists at Kew learned the difficult trick of propagating it in the laboratory and it was saved: dozens of seedlings have now been planted out.

More than can be said for *Cephalanthera rubra*, the red helleborine. This is now critically endangered, it is Britain's most threatened flower, being reduced to three locations only, and it is also exceptionally lovely: the beauty and the rarity combine in an incomparable allure, which is why my heart beat faster and faster as on that hot day at the start of July I stumbled through the Chiltern beechwoods towards it. And I was not disappointed: I gazed and gazed. I trembled with excitement. I wanted to shout for joy. In the Chilterns, for God's sake, in the gentlest of landscapes, what can do that to you in the Chilterns?

Only orchids.

Michael McCarthy, 2016

Duckweed, and some other pond weeds, appear soon after Midsummer, so that stagnant waters are seldom clean during the aestival season. In Aug. and Sept. many ponds and ditches are quite green, like a carpet, with it.

Thomas Furly Forster, The Pocket Encyclopaedia
of Natural Phenomena, *published 1827*

If the regular City man, who leaves Lloyd's at five o'clock, and drives home to Hackney, Clapton, Stamford-hill, or elsewhere, can be said to have any daily recreation beyond his dinner, it is his garden. He never does anything to it with his own hands; but he takes great pride in it notwithstanding; and if you are desirous of paying your addresses to the youngest daughter, be sure to be in raptures with every flower and shrub it contains. If your poverty of expression compel you to make any distinction between the two, we would certainly recommend your bestowing more admiration on his garden than his wine. He always takes a walk round it, before he starts for town in the morning, and is particularly anxious that the fish-pond should be kept specially neat. If you call on him on Sunday in summer-time, about an hour before dinner, you will find him sitting in an arm-chair, on the lawn behind the house, with a straw hat on, reading a Sunday paper. A short distance from him you will most likely observe a handsome paroquet in a large brass-wire cage; ten to one but the two eldest girls are loitering in one of the side walks accompanied by a couple of young gentlemen, who are holding parasols over them – of course only to keep the sun off – while the younger children, with the under nursery-maid, are strolling listlessly about, in the shade. Beyond these occasions, his delight in his garden appears to arise more from the consciousness of possession than actual enjoyment of it. When he drives you down to dinner on a week-day, he is rather fatigued with the occupations of the morning, and tolerably cross into the bargain; but when the cloth is removed, and he has drank three or four glasses of his favourite port, he orders the French windows of his dining-room (which of course look into the garden) to be opened, and throwing a silk handkerchief over his head, and leaning back in his arm-chair, descants at considerable length upon its beauty, and the cost of maintaining it. This is to impress you – who are a young friend of the family – with a due sense of the excellence of the garden, and the wealth of its owner; and when he has exhausted the subject, he goes to sleep.

There is another and a very different class of men, whose recreation is their garden. An individual of this class, resides some short distance from town – say in the Hampstead-road, or the Kilburn-road, or any other road where the houses are small and neat, and have little slips of back garden. He and his wife – who is as clean and compact a little body as himself – have occupied the same house ever since he retired from business twenty years ago. They have no family. They once had a son, who died at about five years old. The child's portrait hangs over the mantelpiece in the best sitting-room, and a little cart he used to draw about, is carefully preserved as a relic.

In fine weather the old gentleman is almost constantly in the garden; and when it is too wet to go into it, he will look out of the window at it, by the hour together. He has always something to do there, and you will see him digging, and sweeping, and cutting, and planting, with manifest delight. In springtime, there is no end to the sowing of seeds, and sticking little bits of wood over them, with labels, which look like epitaphs to their memory; and in the evening, when the sun has gone down, the perseverance with which he lugs a great watering-pot about is perfectly astonishing. The only other recreation he has, is the newspaper, which he peruses every day, from beginning to end, generally reading the most interesting pieces of intelligence to his wife, during breakfast. The old lady is very fond of flowers, as the hyacinth-glasses in the parlour-window, and geranium-pots in the little front court, testify. She takes great pride in the garden too: and when one of the four fruit-trees produces rather a larger gooseberry than usual, it is carefully preserved under a wine-glass on the sideboard, for the edification of visitors, who are duly informed that Mr. So-and-so planted the tree which produced it, with his own hands. On a summer's evening, when the large watering-pot has been filled and emptied some fourteen times, and the old couple have quite exhausted themselves by trotting about, you will see them sitting happily together in the little summerhouse, enjoying the calm and peace of the twilight, and watching the shadows as they fall upon the garden, and gradually growing thicker and more sombre, obscure the tints of their gayest flowers – no bad emblem of the years that have silently rolled over their heads, deadening in their course the brightest hues of early hopes and feelings which have long since faded away. These are their only recreations, and they require no more. They have within themselves, the materials of comfort and content; and the only anxiety of each, is to die before the other.

This is no ideal sketch. There *used* to be many old people of this description; their numbers may have diminished, and may decrease still more. Whether the course female education has taken of late days – whether the pursuit of giddy frivolities, and empty nothings, has tended to unfit women for that quiet domestic life, in which they show far more beautifully than in the most crowded assembly, is a question we should feel little gratification in discussing: we hope not.

Let us turn now, to another portion of the London population, whose recreations present about as strong a contrast as can well be conceived – we mean the Sunday pleasurers; and let us beg our readers to imagine themselves stationed by our side in some well-known rural 'Tea-gardens.'

The heat is intense this afternoon, and the people, of whom there are additional parties arriving every moment, look as warm as the tables which have been recently painted, and have the appearance of being red-hot. What a dust and noise! Men and women – boys and girls – sweethearts and married people – babies in arms, and children in chaises – pipes and shrimps – cigars and periwinkles – tea and tobacco. Gentlemen, in alarming waistcoats, and steel watch-guards, promenading about, three abreast, with surprising dignity (or as the gentleman in the next box facetiously observes, 'cutting it uncommon fat!') – ladies, with great, long, white pocket-handkerchiefs like small table-cloths, in their hands, chasing one another on the grass in the most playful and interesting manner, with the view of attracting the attention of the aforesaid gentlemen – husbands in perspective ordering bottles of ginger-beer for the objects of their affections, with a lavish disregard of expense; and the said objects washing down huge quantities of 'shrimps' and 'winkles,' with an equal disregard of their own bodily health and subsequent comfort – boys, with great silk hats just balanced on the top of their heads, smoking cigars, and trying to look as if they liked them – gentlemen in pink shirts and blue waistcoats, occasionally upsetting either themselves, or somebody else, with their own canes.

Some of the finery of these people provokes a smile, but they are all clean, and happy, and disposed to be good-natured and sociable. Those two motherly-looking women in the smart pelisses, who are chatting so confidentially, inserting a 'ma'am' at every fourth word, scraped an acquaintance about a quarter of an hour ago: it originated in admiration of the little boy who belongs to one of them – that diminutive specimen of mortality in the three-cornered pink satin hat with black feathers. The two men in the blue coats and drab trousers, who are walking up and down, smoking their pipes, are their husbands. The party in the opposite box are a pretty fair specimen of the generality of the visitors. These are the father and mother, and old grandmother: a young man and woman, and an individual addressed by the euphonious title of 'Uncle Bill,' who is evidently the wit of the party. They have some half-dozen children with them, but it is scarcely necessary to notice the fact, for that is a matter of course here. Every woman in 'the gardens,' who has been married for any length of time, must have had twins on two or three occasions; it is impossible to account for the extent of juvenile population in any other way.

Observe the inexpressible delight of the old grandmother, at Uncle Bill's splendid joke of 'tea for four: bread-and-butter for forty;' and the loud explosion of mirth which follows his wafering a paper 'pigtail' on the waiter's collar. The young man is evidently 'keeping company' with Uncle Bill's niece: and Uncle Bill's hints – such as 'Don't forget me at the dinner, you know,' 'I shall look out for the cake, Sally,' 'I'll be godfather to your first – wager it's a boy,' and so forth, are equally embarrassing to the young people, and delightful to the elder ones. As to the old grandmother, she is in perfect ecstasies, and does nothing but laugh herself into fits of coughing, until they have finished the 'gin-and-water warm with,' of which Uncle Bill ordered 'glasses round' after tea, 'just to keep the night air out, and to do it up comfortable and riglar arter sitch an as-tonishing hot day!'

It is getting dark, and the people begin to move. The field leading to town is quite full of them; the little hand-chaises are dragged wearily along, the children are tired, and amuse themselves and the company generally by crying, or resort to the much more pleasant expedient of going to sleep – the mothers begin to wish they were at home again – sweethearts grow more sentimental than ever, as the time for parting arrives – the gardens look mournful enough, by the light of the two lanterns which hang against the trees for the convenience of smokers – and the waiters, who have been running about incessantly for the last six hours, think they feel a little tired, as they count their glasses and their gains.

Charles Dickens, 'London Recreations', 1835

'Daddy, look!' he calls from the top of the slope. 'Sausage lichen!'

It is a rare cloudless blue sky in the middle of the summer, and we are visiting a favourite spot on Dartmoor. Holding a small branch as if it is the most fragile of porcelain sculptures, he runs carefully towards me. There is a subconscious skill in the way he runs down the slope, aware of everything around him: his precious cargo remains safe as he effortlessly dodges the most delicate purple violets, and zig-zags through young ferns unravelling their bright green new fronds, cautious not to trample anything. Perhaps his senses are so astute not because he has super powers, but because he is aware of the natural world all around. He is four and a half years old, but he has an innate respect for nature. And it shines.

He approaches, holding out his prize. The small rugged-looking branch is about as long as my forearm, but this is no ordinary piece of wood. And he knows it. Dangling down, is a soft looking, light green clump; as if an oddly coloured sheep has snagged its wool on the branch.

'And look Daddy, there. Lettuce lichen,' he says excitedly. His subtly creased brow lines reveal his familiar seriousness when he has discovered something he is proud of.

We talk about the wind-broken stick and the lichen that have made their home there. He is hungry and his curiosity needs feeding. His enquiring mind is churning out many questions so he can make sense of this odd thing he has discovered. This clump of an otherwise obscure growth on a broken twig gets us talking about *Peter Rabbit* and the beasts of the last Ice Age in the South West. And why shouldn't it? Lichen is bizarrely wonderful. What makes it so funky is that it is not just one species but two, and sometimes three! In passing, some lichen may seem like a flat, dull, lifeless, crusty thing on a surface, but it is in fact an incredibly complex system of two (or more) organisms living together for mutual gain. Lichen is the Han Solo and Chewbacca of the natural world (with Luke Skywalker occasionally hanging around). This incredible relationship is between single celled algae or cyanobacteria (or sometimes both) and filaments of fungus. It is a truly symbiotic relationship: the algae get the protection from the fungus, and the fungus feeds from algae's photosynthetic food. With no need for roots to take up food, the fungus can grow almost anywhere, from the tops of delicate leaves to in between paving stones beneath your feet. Lichen can grow in some of the most extreme environments on the planet, from the hellishly hot conditions at Yellowstone Park to the freezing, Hoth-like temperatures on Antarctica.

And Peter Rabbit? Well, this is a nice little link. Peter Rabbit and friends were brought to life through the wonderful imagination and glorious illustrations of Beatrix Potter. Her fascination with wildlife didn't stop with anthropomorphising rabbits, frogs and foxes. In incredible detail, Potter painted hundreds of elegant watercolours of fungi and lichen. She was fascinated by these botanical curiosities, and carried out countless experiments to observe how they grew. She even questioned what lichens actually were. However, Potter wasn't the first. Some thirty years before, a Swiss botanist, Simon Schwendener, spent several years looking at the relationship between fungus and algae to explain exactly what lichen is. His ideas about lichen being two separate organisms didn't take root with the British botanical circles, even when Potter tried to reignite Schwendeners' ideas, producing her own unique experiments. Her results, and her views, were ignored. The botanical world in the mid 1890s was not ready for two organisms living as one. Nor was it ready for a female botanist to be explaining what lichens really were, backed by successful experiments.

Little old lichen, inconspicuously alive and elegantly beautiful, is a lifeline for many animals. In harsh winters, the wonderfully shaggy musk ox and the sturdy reindeer scrape lichen off the rocks for food with their strong front incisors. What's more incredible is that, until relatively recently, these beasts were wandering the British landscape: while reindeer trundled along in their huge herds, woolly mammoths lolloped. Reindeer fossils have been found at cave sites across Britain. In the South West of England, around 20,000 to 15,000 years ago, when the climate was much colder, reindeer were scraping lichen off rocks with wolves howling in the distance.

One of the favourite stories my son loves is that some species were used to dye clothes in the past. There is a special ingredient added to lichen which was hand scraped off the cold, hard granite on Dartmoor. The key is in the pee. (The ammonia in the urine brings out the colour from the lichen.) This has been used for hundreds of years all across Europe. A wonderful fact he shares with his little sister.

As we chat my son spots a small weevil moving through the sausage lichen. He holds his breath for what seems like an eternity, for fear of unleashing a terrible gale on this tiny creature. He watches it move each jointed leg incredibly slowly through what must seem like mangrove forests to this enigmatic little beetle. My little one notices everything: the odd, unsynchronised movement of the antennae, the comically disproportionate nose. His brow lines begin to crease again.

Nature captures us so strongly because we all have a natural curiosity with the animals and plants of the world. David Attenborough recognised this, when he wrote, 'Every child in this world has an innate pleasure and delight and interest and curiosity in the natural world.' I would go a step further, and say every *person* in this world has that innate pleasure, delight, interest and curiosity.

That may seem like quite a bold statement, but I have seen it so many times. The reaction of little ones and their parents is so similar when they see a real skeleton up close or come face to face with a pickled octopus, the only difference being that adults are more restrained. But talk to them about the creature, show it to them close, and that inner child comes out pretty quickly. Perhaps as adults our lives are so filled with bills, chores, jobs and other things that we often forget to stop and look at the world around us. Maybe not everyone likes dinosaurs. Not everyone likes trees. But there is *something* about nature that everybody does like.

Look at this wonderful organism, and you will see beautiful colours, with those stunning tiny cups to release its next generation. By looking closer at the lichen, your eyes are seeing more. We might catch a shimmer of blue as an iridescent ground beetle moves nearby, or a blue tit singing on a nearby branch. The world around us is breathtakingly beautiful. The more we look, the more we see that beauty.

Jan Freedman, 2016

The Farne Islands off the Northumbrian coast provide a feast for the senses. There is a smorgasbord of sounds: the calls of innumerable seabirds mingle perfectly with the sounds made by tourists and the rumble of waves against rock. The Farnes are pristine to look at: bleached cliffs, jagged outcrops and shadowed caves; a true wilderness. But it is the smell of these islands that captivates me. The whitened rock, stained by centuries of guano, emits a fantastically fishy odour in the warm summer sun. It is a stench that may be unpleasant to some; to me, it epitomises everything good about the Farnes.

In summertime these islands spring to life as countless seabirds return from their winter habitats. Guillemots and razorbills now bejewel the cliffs, black and brown against the pale rock. The latter, though at first appearing docile, vigorously defend their chicks from marauding gulls, presenting a wall of upturned bills not dissimilar to a medieval spear wall. Another auk, the puffin, is the reason most people visit these islands. The clowns of the avian world, charismatic and confiding, puffins never fail to delight. Whether loafing on the sea or pottering across paths, often with a bill full of shimmering sand eels, they invariably draw a crowd. With some thirty-seven thousand pairs currently residing on the Farnes, visitors are rarely disappointed.

Elsewhere on the imposing cliffs kittiwakes nest en masse, dainty and pristine. The constant 'Kitti-wake', repeated relentlessly, provides a soundtrack to the veritable soap opera unfolding on the cliffs below, where a life-and-death drama takes place under the watchful eye of my favourite seabird, the shag. I challenge anyone to look into the eyes of a shag and not be entranced by their emerald-green hue, which perfectly complements the iridescent sheen of the birds themselves. The young shags may leave a lot to be desired aesthetically – they are prehistoric, reptilian and altogether tatty – but they are still a splendid fixture of the season.

Away from the cliffs things are far from dull; here, on the island tops, a multitude of terns nestle amid historical relics, content and watchful until, of course, you stray too close. An arctic tern in summer is a formidable sight. These marvellous migrants tirelessly pursue all foolish enough to venture nearby – human or gull – putting on a fine show as they dance, swallow-like, in the breeze.

Sadly, all visitors must depart; but, as the boats set sail for shore, grey seals swim within metres of the vessels, their almost canine curiosity matched by the delight of their adoring fans. Eventually, the seals withdraw and the sound of seabirds melts away. But it is worth taking one last backward glance at the impressive sight of the Farnes, framed by the summer sky: rugged, wild, untamed and perfect in their own way.

James Common, 2016

Pausing, the year suspends its drama. The hayfields are empty and silent; the yellow-grey of stubble sinks already below the rising green of the after-grass: for summer thunderstorms have watered the meadows.

July is a time of little events, many and intimate, hidden under the quiet routine of village days. Life tastes good to the cottager this month. The sense of surprise may have gone from it, even as maturity lacks the unexpectedness of youth, and the harvest waits its moment. But there are little heralding harvests that show the way to the fullness of the later year. Go through the village street at twilight when thatched roof and lean-to are blurred against the silver sky. The cottage gardens are dotted with squat, headless ghosts, white against the dusk. Lean over the fence and peer closely and you will see no phantoms, but harmless, old lace curtains swathed round ripening fruit bushes, against the ravaging of birds. For the soft fruit harvest has come again.

Throughout the long evenings of July, the village women bend low in their gardens over raspberry cane and currant bush, gooseberry and loganberry. Time after time, baskets of shining fruit, purple currants and red and yellow gooseberry globes are taken into the gloom of cottage kitchens.

As the women pick the fruit, the men are busy with the vegetables. In this pause between haysel and harvest, when the work on the farm ends at its stated moment of the day, leaving the men free during the summer evenings, it is the gardeners' chance. Tenderly they care for their rule-straight rows of vegetables, staking the swelling peas and beans, watering, hoeing and weeding. Allotments gleam with lines of pale green salads, contrasted with tossing plumes of darker carrot tops; the pods of peas range up and down their staked plants like crotchets on a page of written music. Soon will come the time for the annual Village Show, when the pick of the vegetable gardens for miles around will lie in state, washed and trimmed, under marquees in the Rectory Meadow, and lucky bunches of giant onions or clumps of scrubbed potatoes will proudly bear the blue card of First Prize.

The men work into the night; the sound of the hoe comes from the cabbage patch when it is so dark that nothing shows but the white of the lilies and pinks and the ducks asleep by the pond.

But it is not only the fruit and vegetables that call just now.

The cottage flower garden is the most essentially English thing of our countryside, and this month it flames with blossoms. Bees tumble among the rainbow colours of the herbaceous borders and roses smother cottage porches and darken casement windows. This love of flowers is so strong, that in his cabbage patch the farm labourer will sacrifice some of the limited space to them, and splashes of blue and crimson bloom among onions and beans. Even the village railway station glows with flowers, and the old stationmaster hoes between his rose bushes as he awaits the arrival of the uptrain to London.

It is summer's turning point and everything is full and lush, be it rush of flowers in the gardens or fling of convolvulus over the hedges in the lane, or the milky stream of meadowsweet in the ditches.

The sunny days are hot and heavy with the sound of bees. As the ploughboy goes for his beer at midday to the Black Swan, he pauses and loiters under the bee-covered, flowering lime trees, inarticulately wondering at this beauty of scent and sound. The lanes are full of fledglings that as yet know no fear, while the air is broken by young swallows learning to fly.

But in contrast to all this swift movement of young life, there are the hoers. Six in a line they stand, backs bent in the heat, weeding the rows of swedes in the root fields. Their movements across the field seem so slow as to be hardly perceptible. Six hoes go out at the same angle to weed and thin among the roots; six identical twists of the tool lift the weeds; six pairs of legs move slowly forward. Hour on hour these figures work without word or divergence. The air above them quivers in the heat.

Through the afternoon the cows laze in the sloping meadows. But now it is milking time. They sleepily turn their heads as they hear the cowman lift the latch of the gate. He calls to them across the field.

'Frump; Daisy and Moth; Flossy and Snowdrop; Dapple.'

They swing themselves round like heavy ships and move in orderly line across the meadow. Slowly they saunter over the dry caked mud of the farmyard and each cow goes to her ordained place in the coolness of the whitewashed cowshed. The udders are full and heavy, and the cows are unstinting as they give themselves to the milkers. The men sit on the three-legged stools, peaks of caps turned to the nape of their necks, resting their heads against the hot flanks of the cows. Gently and firmly they pull at the udders and with a light, squirting noise the milk falls in to the pail, foaming with the impact. Soon the cows are all milked, and quietly the orderly line moves out again into the westering sun – Bess and Queenie, Dapple and Snowdrop.

As the month goes on to its close, there is a feeling that the stage is being set for the drama of the harvest. The faint scent of wheat in flower is perceptible no longer, and the fields of grain stand high and firm. The oats are turning silver and there is a warm flush on the wheat.

But there is still time to pause and dally, and on these lengthy summer evenings the youth of the village is free. The lanes are heavy and secret for courting, and as the farm lads walk out with their girls in the long shadowed light, the leafage bends low to hide them. Their murmuring is broken by shouts from the village green, where the local cricket team is playing a neighbouring village. Under the bordering elms the old men sit to watch the game.

The evening air grows cooler. Outside their cottage doors sit the aged people. In the dusk their white aprons and white shirtsleeves show in the gardens like clumps of white blossom. Silently they sit, hour after hour, with tired hands at rest on their laps and eyes looking quietly around them at the swallows nesting in their thatch, or the cat asleep under the roses, or the gold in the sky.

Night falls upon the village very gently.

Clare Leighton, The Farmer's Year:
A Calendar of English Husbandry, *1933*

S ummer holidays at my uncle's were a family tradition – start-ing with my nan, then later bringing my dad and his brother, and then at last, me. My uncle's garden was a nature lover's para-dise. I'd been told hundreds of stories about it. He had a pond with water voles plopping into it and grass snakes sunbathing on its banks, so I was excited when it was my turn to explore.

The first day of our summer holiday was over so quickly, and we sat in the garden absorbing the atmosphere and watching the sky gradually turn red while we tucked into fish and chips. It was well deserved after a day of garden adventures, but I was too full of that fresh air and excitement to eat much. At home I'd take leftovers with me on my evening walk, as a late snack for the badgers or foxes I hoped to watch or film overnight with my trail camera. The pungent smell is perfect to attract any nocturnal or shy creatures lurking locally and I knew that nature wouldn't be sleeping in my uncle's garden after sunset.

I had examined every minor detail of this patch during the day, but didn't find any tell-tale signs of what creatures might be there. No corridors cutting low in the hedge, no badger latrine, no nostril blowing scents of a fox, not even footprints in the wet mud. I became all the more eager to learn what would happen when lights were out and the garden resumed its usual silence.

I wasn't the only one who was up before sunrise, impatient to see what had been captured during the night on the trail cam-era. As I loaded the video clips on to my laptop my uncle peered over my shoulder, amazed by the use of technology and thrilled by the three elegant animals that had come to finish off our tea. Two young and their mother. The adult vixen trotted along the far view of the camera frame with her nose buried in the grass, sniffing but taking nothing. Looking straight up to the camera for a split second, her eyes glowed. She was slim but healthy, a lean shape typical of a rural fox. Staying back, almost out of frame, she concluded that the area was safe. She then called to where she'd emerged, and immediately her two young burst in and ran straight for the scattered feast.

Foxes are mostly, though not exclusively, nocturnal and are shy; these rural creatures were more timid than their city cousins might be. An opportunity of food like this is also rare for them, although judging by the way the two cubs were scrambling over each other they certainly enjoyed it. Both of them took overly generous mouthfuls, as though they hadn't eaten for days. They stuffed down as much as they could, taking little notice of each other or their surroundings, so it was a good job mum was on the look out.

Before long most of the food had been eaten and a fight broke out, heads clashing as they wrestled for the remnants. Using his back legs the larger sibling pushed the other out of the way, spreading his legs over the other's back and trapping him. His brother tried to escape by shaking vigorously and squealing, his bushy tail going round in circles. Eventually the mother vixen intervened and split up a squabble that was also a fight for the best feed – vital for their future.

Before it was all gone the mother pushed the cubs out of the way, who sat and watched while she took her share, one of them gently grooming her. Throughout, the vixen remained on high alert, at one point gazing alertly into the distance before continuing to eat. The cubs were only about four to five months old but we could see how they were developing into independence within their environment. As one of the cubs wandered off we noticed that it had a limp – not ideal when living in the wild as there's no time for resting.

They all had delightful personalities, though. My uncle, leaning over my shoulder to watch the video clips, was clearly fascinated. Then he said, 'They used to take the chickens from the orchard when your nan was younger.'

Georgia Locock, 2016

Poised in the middle of the water, the mother mallard gave away his presence, and I instantly understood her panic when a brief eel-line of darkness broke the surface. Like her, I thought the otter was trying to seize her one surviving duckling, and I realised as she thrashed down the dyke that she was attempting to lure him away.

The otter surfaced twice, its broad head sitting squat upon the waterline, and then all went quiet. I followed gingerly along the dyke edge and within seconds there it was: a dark shape feeding lengthwise along the bank. At just five metres away I could hear every crunch of bone and the soft chafing sound of those long white teeth working the flesh. There was an open-mouthed relish to the way he gulped down his evening meal, but it was not a duckling, as I'd anticipated; it was a fresh pike. In the time it took to reach the spot, he'd caught the fish and eaten most of the body. He toyed briefly with the final morsel, but fish heads were not to his magisterial taste and, casting me a quick glance as he slipped back into the water, he continued fishing in an unhurried departure.

I never saw more than the head again. But the effect of his passage was as if electricity had been run down the length of the dyke and a shock administered to the whole stretch. The stems of reedmace shuddered with his subaquatic probing and the zigzagging lines of bubbles seemed to solidify on their journey upwards, breaking the surface like fragments of ice.

When the water resumed its customary stillness I went round to inspect the pike and the glass-splinter teeth inside its empty head. I didn't so much walk home. I seemed to float across the marsh by moonlight, and when I finally went to hang up my coat there was just the faintest trace of fishiness on my fingertips.

14 July 2008

Mark Cocker, Claxton: Field Notes from a Small Planet, *2014*

Nature Trail

At the bottom of my garden
There's a hedgehog and a frog
And a lot of creepy-crawlies
Living underneath a log,
There's a baby daddy long legs
And an easy-going snail
And a family of woodlice,
All are on my nature trail.

There are caterpillars waiting
For their time to come to fly,
There are worms turning the earth over
As ladybirds fly by,
Birds will visit, cats will visit
But they always chose their time
And I've even seen a fox visit
This wild garden of mine.

Squirrels come to nick my nuts
And busy bees come buzzing
And when the night time comes
Sometimes some dragonflies come humming,
My garden mice are very shy
And I've seen bats that growl

And in my garden I have seen
A very wise old owl.

My garden is a lively place
There's always something happening,
There's this constant search for food
And then there's all that flowering,
When you have a garden
You will never be alone
And I believe we all deserve
A garden of our own.

Benjamin Zephaniah, 2001

One of my favourite summer adventures began when I heard that a bird I'd read so much about, in books and on the internet, had been seen near Cumbria. For a young bird lover living in North Yorkshire, this was the most amazing news. And this lovely bird? The fantastic European bee-eater.

So why am I so passionate about these birds? Because they're so colourful, bright and vibrant – yellows, blues, even reds. I love kingfishers too, but these are even more spectacular. As they dart through the air you see their beautiful colours as they catch insects with ease. They hardly ever nest in England; Cumbria is the furthest north they have been known to breed. I just had to go and see if I would be lucky enough to see one.

My dad drove me up there. It took two hours but we went through some incredible countryside on the way. We go to Cumbria regularly throughout the year but this was an area of northern Cumbria we didn't really know, so it gave us the chance to follow a different route. We had visited High Force before, but after that it was uncharted territory. I'd never been any further into Upper Teesdale but wow – it was an amazing experience. The hills were beautifully green in most places, and the farm houses dotted around were all painted white. It occurred to me how lovely these hills would be with a 'light dusting of icing'. Snowy caps would look stunning with the luscious green of the grass, and the waterfalls trickling down the sides of the mossy cliff faces. It was utterly beautiful just looking across the valley to the other hills. The road was exciting too, twisting and turning on the hillsides, opening up the full beauty of the countryside. As it was a warm day we had the windows down and you could hear the streams tumbling down the hillsides and smell the hay which had just been cut – it's remarkable how that smell triggers memories of places visited during the summer months. The next time I smell it I'm sure I'll think of this journey.

When we arrived at the village near where the bee-eaters had been seen we got a little confused as there was an RSPB Reserve about a mile away, but we eventually found our way to the bee-eater station, where quite a few people had already gathered. We went through the gates to the quarry and parked up to start the walk to where they were nesting. This was great on its own. As it was summer, everywhere was alive with insects. You could hear the trilling of grasshoppers, dragonflies darted around the edges of pools, and hoverflies and bees covered the wild flowers by the side of the path. Then way up above was the mewing of buzzards. It was a magical experience in every way.

After a bit of a walk we managed to get to their base where a little shelter had been set up at the place where you could best see them. After looking for a while, and with a little help from the volunteers there, I managed to find one with a telescope. When I first saw the bee-eaters through the telescope, they looked even more astonishing than they had when I had seen them in the books. I was so excited when I saw them; it was one of the most amazing moments of my life. They didn't even make any sounds which made them even more enchanting; their stunningly bright colours were the only advertisement they needed. They are spectacular: bright blues, yellows and reds. It's as if someone took the colours of kingfishers, yellowhammers and robins and put them all together.

I couldn't believe I'd seen them. I was absolutely over the moon – and it hadn't taken long at all. I felt such a huge sense of achievement – such a buzz. And when I started to photograph them it got even better. There weren't just bee-eaters there – I managed to get a shot of a great-spotted woodpecker, a wren and a bee-eater all in the same photo!

There is no way of knowing when they will be back again, so I spent a good while watching them. They are fantastic in flight and very quick, darting about catching food and disappearing into their tunnel nest in the sand wall of the quarry. They have a clever trick, too. When they catch a bee, they rub its backside on a branch to get rid of the sting. They catch other insects too, including butterflies and I even got a photo of a bee-eater with a dragonfly in its mouth.

Summer any year is fantastic but I will always think of this day when you say summer. It was an incredible experience from start to finish, and a day I will remember for ever.

Zach Haynes, 2016

The Aestival Season begins about St. Swithin's day, July 15th, and continues till Michaelmas. It is on the whole the hottest season of the year, but the heat gradually declines, and towards the close of the period the nights begin to get cold, and the daily temperature to be much diminished. It is in this season, and particularly in August, that the most beautiful and picturesque skies are seen, and that small meteors most abound; the landscapes too have a peculiar softness of colouring not seen at any other time. As the Solstitial Period is called the early summer, so this season is called the late summer. If it set in with showery weather the chances are that the greater part of the period will be showery, and hence the popular proverb which ascribes forty days' rain to St. Swithin. When the weather is fair in this season the mornings often become gradually more and more obscured by the stratus of the foregoing night.

One remarkable circumstance in this season is the silence of the grove, nearly every bird ceasing to sing, and continuing mute till near the close of the season, when they begin to sing a little again. Many birds now begin by degrees to congregate, and to form large flocks ranging the corn fields together. Starlings are flocked by the end of July, and Linnets by the middle of September; the Swifts leave us about the festival of the Assumption, Aug. 15th, and nothing but an accidental straggler is to be seen left behind.

The fruits of the Aestival Period are delicious. Currants and Gooseberries get quite ripe about the beginning of July, and the various summer Pears, Apricots, Plums, Peaches, Nectarines, and Melons follow; it is indeed the season of fruits, and at no time does Pomona make a greater show than in this season, which before it closes exhibits the orchard in its perfection. In our climate the Vine is not yet productive of ripe Grapes, but in the south of Europe they are gathered early in September.

The aestival Flora cannot be mentioned as the most beautiful of the year, though if well managed a great display of colours may be produced in the garden; the Dahlias, China Asters, French and African Marigolds, Chrysanthemums, Sunflowers, and a great variety of other syngenecious plants flower during this period, and many of them continue till late in autumn. In the fields the flowering of the yellow autumnal Dandelion *Apargia autumnalis*, gives to certain meadows the appearance of a second spring.

Thomas Furly Forster, The Pocket Encyclopaedia
of Natural Phenomena, *published 1827*

In winter the castle is cold and grey, an empty memento of monarchs long gone. In spring the colours begin to soften and spread as trickles of visitors and occasional wedding parties bring back life and warmth and flowers start to bloom. By summer St Mawes is transformed as tourists and tour groups invade; but they are not the only visitors taking advantage of English Heritage's hospitality. Pause the audio guide and look up. Blue iridescent streaks fly overhead, aerodynamic shapes darting from archway to nest and back again without a second thought for the people below: swallows, the returning kings of the castle.

They are a brazen bunch. They do not respectfully hide out of sight or revere Henry VIII's architecture; instead they make it their own and stretch their wings in the grounds, hunting insects by the amber illuminations that wash over their home, this beacon on the coastline. Campaigners for hirundines like swallows and martins will quickly tell you that the reason we see fewer and fewer of them these days is a lack of appropriate housing. In St Mawes the swallows highlight this fact by temporarily occupying one of the oldest, grandest buildings available, certainly grander than any property that a second-home owner could hope to find beside Falmouth Bay. It is the ideal place to raise their young because of the architecture, but also because of the insect life.

It's when they search for food that they treat St Mawes to the best views of themselves, and they go all out to give everyone a good show, skimming close to the ferries on the river, darting through the sheep field and dancing in the sky as they weave around chimneys and other birds. The odd hovering kestrel is encouraged to move on by a daring individual while other hungry mouths swoop overhead. You see, while the swallows may be the kings of the castle, there is also a different colony nearby that is drawn to this waterside location for its ideal accommodation, great views and tasty local produce – that of house martins. Walk from the harbour to the castle on a sunny July evening and you will be greeted by them first, calling and feasting around the cottages. Eventually the swallows appear and the sky becomes truly alive with noise and activity as the two species weave between each other with speed and dexterity. Naturally, some of the humans below simply point up and say 'Oh, look at the swallows,' blind to the differences – such a shame for the handsome little bird that may not have its cousin's colours and sleek shape but is arguably more attractive. And what about the swift? If the glimpse of a blue sheen and forked tail is the sight of summer's arrival, then the scream of a swift has to be the sound. Then there is their shape and speed, the long boomerang that lets them glide high above the village fields, away from the drama at the castle, and always brings them swooping back around again.

All summer the swallow chicks are growing and the evening flights are a common occurrence. By August the noise and frenzy are slowly dying down and the tourists have grown used to sharing the space, but they have yet to master the art of capturing these birds on film. Just as you think you have one coming into view and in focus, it tricks you and changes direction. As the village and its summer visitors gather on sea walls and in fields to marvel at the annual display of the Red Arrows over Falmouth

Docks, they are treated to a warm-up act of avian acrobatics, only this display of speed and agility has become so frequent that just a handful of us still stop to look up and admire it.

Just as soon as we have got used to their presence, they are thinking about departing. Juveniles move from the nest and adults, a job well done, embark on a solitary journey, seemingly abandoning the brood to fend for themselves. It is an ongoing pattern of Cornwall to Africa, back and forth, this year only momentarily broken by an evening catching insects over a 'Colorado saloon', the humans having been drawn into the castle grounds by the travelling theatre and the moths by the theatre's lighting. If you are lucky, in those final weeks you can see a bemused fledgling perched nearby, a little downy feather here or there, looking at its enormous summer residence and contemplating the even longer journey ahead. Up the hill adults linger in long lines on telephone wires, finally providing that ideal photographic opportunity for those who have had the patience to wait for it.

Before we know it the last of the swallows will have gone, the skies around St Mawes Castle will become quiet again and the tide of visitors will ebb away. We will head into the autumn of occasional sunny weekends and history field trips for the new school classes, then back into the emptiness of winter, when the castle, for ever imposing against the south-west skyline, silently awaits the return of its avian kings next summer.

Dawn Bradley, 2016

Here

Swerving east, from rich industrial shadows
And traffic all night north; swerving through fields
Too thin and thistled to be called meadows,
And now and then a harsh-named halt, that shields
Workmen at dawn; swerving to solitude
Of skies and scarecrows, haystacks, hares and pheasants,
And the widening river's slow presence,
The piled gold clouds, the shining gull-marked mud,

Gathers to the surprise of a large town:
Here domes and statues, spires and cranes cluster
Beside grain-scattered streets, barge-crowded water,
And residents from raw estates, brought down
The dead straight miles by stealing flat-faced trolleys,
Push through plate-glass swing doors to their desires -
Cheap suits, red kitchen-ware, sharp shoes, iced lollies,
Electric mixers, toasters, washers, driers –

A cut-price crowd, urban yet simple, dwelling
Where only salesmen and relations come
Within a terminate and fishy-smelling
Pastoral of ships up streets, the slave museum,
Tattoo-shops, consulates, grim head-scarfed wives;
And out beyond its mortgaged half-built edges

SUMMER

Fast-shadowed wheat-fields, running high as hedges,
Isolate villages, where removed lives

Loneliness clarifies. Here silence stands
Like heat. Here leaves unnoticed thicken,
Hidden weeds flower, neglected waters quicken,
Luminously-peopled air ascends;
And past the poppies bluish neutral distance
Ends the land suddenly beyond a beach
Of shapes and shingle. Here is unfenced existence:
Facing the sun, untalkative, out of reach.

Philip Larkin, 1964

The coast has a special place in Britain's natural history. We celebrate our coasts as part of our maritime history and culture, but they are also one of the last places where we can truly experience wild nature, from the phenomenal sea states our winter storms serve up to the pleasure of experiencing a warm moment on a sheltered cliff-side in early spring, where the year's first brimstone butterfly might appear. Summer at the coast, though, has the power to dazzle us, to knock us down with its beauty, to inspire us and fill us with life.

In 1989 – a glorious, hot, dry summer, with day after day of endless sunshine – I was in the West Country, and as part of my Masters degree I was searching for a very obscure and rare plant: the shore dock, a woody member of the dock family which could only be found, more or less, on the beaches of Devon and Cornwall. Visually unbecoming, but fascinating in its ecological lunacy, it is very long-lived, requires a constant supply of fresh water, but its seeds depend on the tide and the sea itself to disperse. It germinates on bare ground created by storm or stream, ground that inevitably disappears as other plants colonise it. The shore dock is therefore forced to adopt the lifestyle of a marine wanderer, appearing in one place for a few years, then being scoured out by a winter storm and popping up elsewhere.

I spent that glorious summer living in a static caravan. As the weeks of sun sped past, and holidaymakers came and went, I was a small, fixed point amid their comings and goings. Each day my quest took me up, down, and along cliff paths, following fishermen's tracks that disappeared into the bracken, taking precipitous drops down to little-visited coves and beaches dotted along the coast. There were bucket-and-spade seaside beaches along which I strode purposefully, clipboard in hand, followed by curious and quizzical children with plastic buckets and spades. Many beaches had been rendered inhospitable to the shore dock: those where streams were culverted, or where cliffs of slumping clay had been tamed, revetted, or clothed in concrete. I discovered that it was beaches which were hardest to reach, with the steepest, slippiest paths, where shore dock survived best. Some, not entirely coincidentally, were also nudist beaches, and as I clambered around with my camera and binoculars I would studiously try to avoid eye contact.

While searching for this obscure plant I found myself, almost by osmosis, learning the other plants of cliffs and beach, of oozing flush and strandline. I grew to appreciate the tenacity of the common reed, which could, with its spreading carpet of roots, create a stable soil from the flotsam washed up and deposited on the beach in winter storms. It was always a pleasure to find the diminutive brookweed, which seemed to relish the challenge of finding the thinnest ledge of a tide-washed rockface on which to grow. There seemed some affinity between the brookweed and the shore dock, as discovering the small white-flowered brookweed seemed to presage discovering a new population of dock – or at least that's how it seemed at the time. Perhaps I had found a totem, a floral talisman, which would help me with my search.

My search took me into another world: the world of plants and their communities, one which I have never, since then, quite left. From time to time I still pay a visit, and give my respects to the wild places where the shore dock lives. I'll continue to do that as long as my knees allow me to descend those vertiginous fishermen's paths.

Miles King, 2016

I was on my way into town when I first saw them stumbling out of a hedge onto the street. It was a sunny morning, still and close and about to become hot later. There had been days of this: an uncharacteristically hot and clammy July, not like recent British monsoon summers, although there was a shower last week. Nothing unusual on the street: some morning shoppers buying veg from under the Guildhall, cakes from the baker's, queuing outside the butcher's, fetching newspapers; a few visitors taking photographs, walking dogs; swifts gangling over the bell tower, jackdaws in churchyard trees and the yaffle, a green woodpecker, shouting at sheep in fields beyond the priory. The town was behaving normally for a sunny Saturday morning, oblivious to the metropolis about to spill out from under its hedges and pavements. All I needed from the ironmonger's was some 13 amp fuses, perhaps symbolic of an electrifying moment about to spark up. I rushed back to check my own back garden. They were there too, the pismires: *piss* because their colonies drenched in formic acid smell like urine and more from the Latin name for ant. They were flying ants.

This was the moment, at least a moment, when quite separate ant colonies synchronised their nuptial flight. In this case, the distance between my garden colony and the one I'd seen under the hedge in town was about 100 yards. There would be others scattered around too, perhaps in other towns, other counties, doing the same thing. At the edge of our garden path, under a fringe of red deadnettle, the black ants were pouring out of the nest. At first they were all piling on top of each other as if in panic, a scrabbling, chaotic, mass. It appeared haphazard at first but it soon became obvious that it was organised and purposeful. Tiny worker ants were running protectively around the perimeter while many others seemed to be coaxing the alates – the winged offspring – into the light. First came the drones – the tiny winged males – then the gynes or virgin queens emerged, twice the size of the drones. They all appeared to blunder around drunkenly together until they got the idea of climbing up the plant stems. There was no hanky-panky before take-off, perhaps an obvious strategy to prevent interbreeding, but how these things are determined is a mystery known only to the swarm mind.

The theory is that nuptial flights are triggered by weather fronts creating warm, still flying conditions a few days after rain has softened the earth for queens to burrow into and start new colonies. This is certainly true this year: it is still, warm and humid. In recent years the idea of Flying Ant Day – when all the black ants swarm at once – has been extended into several days in July and August perhaps because the kinds of weather fronts the ants need have been disrupted by other fronts bringing rain. In 2012, a survey carried out by the Society of Biology listed 6,000 reports of flying ants over a two-week period in Britain. In the hot but sporadic summer of 2013, there were four separate flying ant days, the first in June and the last in September. This summer it seems the ants 'know' there is better weather and what's more they've been preparing for it.

Each nuptial flight involves many colonies and many millions of individuals. How they all perceive ideal weather conditions and act upon it together on the same day suggests communication and planning. A black ant colony can contain 15,000 workers, although smaller colonies of 4,000–7,000 are more common. This Shropshire market town has a population of around 3,000 people in an area of a few hectares. If there was only one black ant nest for each of the 1,400 households, it would mean, at a very conservative estimate, a population of 5,600,000 ants occupying the same space as the people. In reality the total black ant population would be many millions more and, until the nuptial flight, coexist almost invisibly with the human inhabitants. Natural phenomena can still arouse fierce passions. Confronted by something they don't understand and which strikes them as weird, disgusting and on their doorstep, a common response is for people to reach for the Ant Doom – *destroy complete ant colonies without trace . . . discrete and easy to use* – or pour a kettle of boiling water over the seething insects. Catering for this impulse to annihilate the other population of our town, the ironmonger sells a large selection of weapons of mass destruction: smoke bombs, electrocution devices, poison pens, sprays, powders, granules, swats.

I find swarms fascinating, a collective consciousness, like watching a mind thinking. My wife Nancy and I were walking on Wenlock Edge, trying to decide whether to buy a house here when we jokingly agreed we would make the decision based on a sign. Within half an hour we were engulfed in the roar of a thousand wings as a swarm of bees passed overhead and gathered in the branches of a beech tree. We walked right through the swarm; it was electrifying and strangely humbling. We bought the house. Of course I've been stung many times by wasps, occasionally by bees and once had a painful run-in with a swarm of white-faced hornets in America. I have watched murmurations of starlings and clouds of bats in awe. I sympathise with poor farmers enduring a locust migration of biblical proportions but see in the plague a savage beauty. Even more terrifying, I have seen colonies of bacteria swarm into infection or disease proportions under a microscope but feel oddly inspired by them. I don't think this is necessarily a perverse reaction yet it does run counter to the revulsion of the swarm shared by many in Western society. However, human social attitudes, particularly to social insects, are ambiguous.

The work ethic and selfless sociability of ants may be admired as qualities of fascinating but mindless automatons until the robots appear intentional. Hundreds of ants marching across your kitchen floor and getting, literally or metaphorically, in your pants, quickly provokes ecophobia which is fundamental to preserving civilisation. 'Buzz Off! Family forced to eat under a mosquito net after swarms of flies invade Avonmouth' (*Daily Mail*). 'Beemageddon – school closed, shoppers attacked and car covered as swarm of bees cause chaos' (*Mirror*). 'Thousands of Wasps Found in UK Home Devouring Bed' (*abc News*). 'Ginormous Jellyfish Swarm England' (*gogo News*). Swarms represent Nature out of control. There is a tipping pint into panic somewhere between many and too many, any large number of ants, bees, jellyfish, toads, bats, sparrows or locusts.

This horror of the swarm might have to do with the sheer numbers of creatures in one place or doing something strange when a lesser number of the same thing would appear beautiful. Take mayflies: they spend a year in the mud of slow-moving rivers and streams, moulting through different stages until the adults all hatch together, then they take to the air to mate, the females lay eggs in the river and they are all dead in forty-eight hours. One spring, Nancy and I went to Ironbridge to see the River Severn when the water level was at an all-time low. As tyres screeched along the Wharfage, we dropped down behind the car park into a silent cloud of mayflies, glimmering with golden light above the water. By the time the sun set behind the cooling towers of the power station, the swarm had vanished, washed downriver. The next morning felt like a change in the seasons and by afternoon a gang of swifts were screaming around the church tower – they had come back from their travels. The swifts brought new weather and a soft, scent-releasing rain. The suddenness in the sky was charged with swashbuckling clouds and a rain of mad birds, gold swarms and iridescent wings. These things were not just loose ephemera but essential elements of a seasonal shift which opened the sky to summer.

Paul Evans, Field Notes from the Edge, *2015*

The day starts disconcertingly, with small frogs being flushed out of the cold water tap. The water supply comes from a spring on the hill behind the house and it is sealed by a concrete lid. I can only assume the frogs gain entry by climbing up the long grass stems and into the overflow pipe. They obviously spawn there and leave by the same route. Around the pools and lakes at this time of the year the grass is often alive with such tiny frogs, only recently emerged from their aquatic domain. Herons are quick to avail themselves of such an easy meal without having to undergo the usual patient waiting for fish. In the field below the spring, I can see two of them stalking stiffly through the long grass like tall and slender ballet dancers, stabbing every so often into the ground.

This hasn't been a good year at all. Despite the promise of a warm and dry spring and summer, it has been cool and wet – catastrophic for ground-nesting birds and fledglings. Today is no different, beginning with light showers broken by the odd sunny spell. I utilize the longer breaks to weed the rockery of some of the more rampant of the wild plants: rosebay willow herb, dandelion and herb robert, buttercups and nettles, but leave the vetch, bilberry, teasel and, of course, the wild strawberries. Weeding is easy on this soil, because it is finely crumbled rock, like a coarse sand and the roots come away easily. Among the rosebay I discover a fat elephant hawk moth caterpillar with its large painted 'eyes' to frighten-off predators.

Late afternoon, during a lull, I stroll up the valley road, past the old lead mine. The ruins of the roofless winding house

149

with its crumbling walls looks like a smashed skull, with ferns growing from window-orifices. On the hill behind it, sheep are ascending slowly in single file like humble pilgrims departing a shrine. One of the fields close by has the appearance of a green firmament, speckled with white starts, which on closer inspection turn out to be fresh horse mushrooms. They provide a wonderful side-dish for dinner that evening, after I discard the few riddled with grubs.

Both the following days and nights bring continuous heavy showers and strong blustery winds; the sky lies on the hills like armour plate – heavy and oppressive. It is such a pity that the weather is so obstinate because the hills are looking their best now, with a light purple dusting of heather, interspersed with freckles of chrome-yellow gorse and a touch here and there of pastel blue harebells and mauve of betony. There is a good crop of bilberries this year and, despite the rain, I manage to fill two sandwich boxes in under an hour from one small patch above the fir line.

I don waterproofs and climb the north-eastern ridge. The stream is as full as in winter and rushes in torrents down the valley; the ground is as leaky as a colander and water trickles out of every pore and crevice. I climb up through the hanging oakwood which extends up from the road and then through the bracken, following the sheep tracks, slipping and sliding as I try to maintain my foothold. Three buzzards are circling above me, one of them mewing. They are probably hungry and are utilising a lull in the weather to take wing again. A female kestrel hovers below me, with what looks like a jess dangling from its leg.

Over the lakes a lone kite is circling, while a little below on the hillside leading into the lakes two men are inserting fence posts. Their hammering reverberates around the valley like a loud expletive in a gentlemen's club. The fencing, too, in its strict geometry of containing lines offends against nature's anarchy. The farmer has cleared the whole hillside of its rich gorse and bracken scrub and reseeded it with fescue grass and root crop for the sheep.

Four ravens plunge over the brow of the hill, croaking with annoyance at the intruding figures. A pair of mistle thrushes feed readily on the freshly planted ground and a female wheatear rummages among an overlooked clump of large thistles on one of which a painted lady butterfly is languidly flapping. As I pass the oak wood by the cottage I'm surprised to hear a wood warbler trilling, but the song is snapped off like a twig before completion, as the bird realises it's pointless now. The sky is now clear and the western horizon tugs at a sun reluctant to vacate the cloying blue.

23 July

John Green, Wings Over the Valley: A Bird Watcher's Wales Diary, *2000*

Summer Dawn

Pray but one prayer for me 'twixt thy closed lips,
Think but one thought of me up in the stars.
    The summer night waneth, the morning light slips,
Faint & grey 'twixt the leaves of the aspen, betwixt the
    cloud-bars,
That are patiently waiting there for the dawn:
    Patient and colourless, though Heaven's gold
Waits to float through them along with the sun.
Far out in the meadows, above the young corn,
    The heavy elms wait, and restless and cold
The uneasy wind rises; the roses are dun;
Through the long twilight they pray for the dawn.
Round the lone house in the midst of the corn.
Speak but one word to me over the corn,
Over the tender, bow'd locks of the corn.

William Morris, published 1858

A sk a child to draw a butterfly. Chances are they won't design a 'little brown job' – a gatekeeper or a meadow brown. Commas are a bit ragged around the edges and what about dingy or grizzled skippers? Sounds more like the name of a dodgy bar or salt-crusted old fisherman, than a delicately marked little insect.

Instead, let their imaginations take them on a journey through colours and shapes and textures. Add detail, make it elegant, make it showy and ostentatious: draw a butterfly as you would like to see one dancing among bright flowers and swaying grasses.

Perhaps you'll start to get close to the swallowtail butterfly *Papilio machaon (britannicus)*.

Butterfly watching is the perfect way to while away a fragrant, hot afternoon. First of all, butterflies like the sunshine – warm, dry days – the kind associated with sipping Pimm's in the back garden, mowing the lawn, barbeques on the patio and the slightly flat notes of an approaching ice cream van. Butterflies love long days with tuneful mornings and colourful sunsets that last until midnight. They enjoy gentle breezes and the rich smell of pollen filling the air.

These particular butterflies happen to inhabit very beautiful places, too. Swallowtails are one of our rarest butterflies, making their home in small pockets of the vast and waterlogged Norfolk Broads. Their range is restricted in the UK by the availability of milk-parsley on which they lay their eggs and their habitat has diminished over recent years. Strumpshaw Fen, Hickling Broad and Ranworth Broad, however, remain strongholds for the swallowtail.

You mustn't be impatient, either; devote an entire lazy afternoon to your quest. This is yet another excuse to savour precious summer days.

Begin your wander through woodlands. Investigate sunlit clearings where the earth is dappled with gold: warm and sheltered and safe. You're not just looking for swallowtails today. Pause and sweep the area carefully, looking for movements – there. A black beauty takes to the air and drifts atop the brambles. The white admiral stands out with the same timelessness of a little black dress, with just a simple white band across the wings: understated and classic.

Continue your walk out into the meadows and reedbeds. If you're lucky a grasshopper warbler will start up. With head raised high and twisting slowly left to right, this little bird sounds like a fishing reel being let out. A plop in a nearby dyke might alert you to a water vole – and don't forget to keep a sharp eye out for the dragonflies.

Chocolate-coloured Norfolk hawkers prowl along the edge of the water, while stately emperors roam imposingly. Chasers, darters and skimmers skirt merrily across the water's surface and the banded demoiselle abounds.

Take breaks regularly – this is gruelling exercise after all. Explore the wildflower beds rich in pollen and buzzing with bees. Another movement – this one, though, is the quintessential buddleia butterfly: the peacock. Like a real peacock, it's flamboyant enough – large, ruby red with a spectacular pattern of purple-blue 'eyes' on the wing, but you may not have noticed it at first. With wings closed, it is nothing more than a dead leaf, but when slowly opened an inner and unexpected beauty is revealed.

The afternoon may be wearing on, but don't despair. The

swallowtail won't be rushed. It'll take to the wing when it's good and ready and not one moment before. Lean against the wooden boardwalks and cast your eye over a large bed of tangled nettles, grasses and summer wildflowers.

Something catches your eye. A large – larger than expected – shape lifts languidly into the air. The peacock makes a random flight, as if suddenly startled. The white admiral goes gliding across the clearing with scarcely a flap of the wing. This creature is larger and more powerful. It skims across the top of the vegetation before dropping down on to a flower – almost out of sight. It flaps its wings frenetically to hold itself steady as it feeds and then moves into full view with wings outstretched.

This is the butterfly of a child's imagination.

Almost ten centimetres across, the black borders of the wings slope gently backwards as it perches. A golden, creamy yellow fills the centre of the wings and the tail curves down elegantly into two points, much like the fork in a swallow's tail. It's exquisitely shaded in midnight blue, as if by an artist's hand, and a large red dot sits dead centre.

Another one joins it and you watch the pair circle over the greenery, their wings looking as if they have absorbed the richness of the summer sun.

Before long, the butterflies have settled and it's time to move on. The sun is hot on your back and it's a fair walk. The grasshopper warbler starts up again, acting as a guide. The air is alive with the hum of insects all busy in their own way. You're not busy though – just satisfied.

You've earned that glass of Pimm's.

Lucy McRobert, 2016

Now, it's summer and the city's loud with the calls of swifts and gulls. A new season, a new ecology of sound. With each season we gain or lose in the vast, global avian exchange of house martin and goose, sanderling and oystercatcher. Each migrating bird carries with it something of ourselves, our sense of memory perhaps, our circannual response to sight and voice.

Summer itself is a concept which seems to shift and spin – here, all the seasons seem mutable – warmth or cold depend on where you've come from, where you're going. For seabirds and waders flown from the Arctic, it's summer in December.

Here in the northeast of Scotland we tell ourselves that, after the privations of winter, we deserve a decent summer, as if there's some transcendent meteorological structure of punishment and reward. In fact, summer's just another season which – like everywhere else – may appear reluctantly or not at all. Occasionally though, it's sudden and glorious in glittering sunrises on the sea-edge, a few rare, hot mornings which will be paid for in the *haar* which by afternoon, will have slid over the city as a damp white net of salty chill. You can become lost in the seasons, disorientated like birds primed for migration too early by unseasonal temperatures or, after a few cold, lightless days of raining grey, preparing inwardly for hibernation, even in July. (Which month is it? When is Christmas?) In our summer, there's an undertow of anxiety, a small voice somewhere telling us to grasp the moment, for the moment won't be long.

The short-eared owls I've been watching all winter and

spring will probably have left. I haven't been to see them for weeks but by now, in response to temperature or hunger or the mysterious, powerful force of Zugunruhe – migratory restlessness – they may already have gone.

It's not just among birds – there's an urgent, unstoppable human Zugunruhe too, manifest at this time of year in crowded airports and quiet streets. Even in the heart of the city, the roads are almost empty. The 4x4s will be silent until August.

In these tranquil weeks, there's a mild, post-apocalyptic feel, a sense both exciting and melancholy of something being different. It seems natural to turn the world asunder, to imagine it always like this, the sounds of humans replaced by the sounds of birds in a radical re-population, an establishment, or re-establishment of rights. It's the way things ought be, not how they really are. Walking through the streets, you walk through warm sea breeze and gull-song.

For months, the gulls have been demonstrating their mighty, operatic passions from their ancestral rooftops, sending arias down the deep granite walls to rise in echo through the streets and lanes. Now, in culmination of long weeks of re-uniting, nesting, mating, young gulls stumble and flap on the roads or lie as small, feathered corpses in the gutters. (Which destination is so urgent as to be worth the life of an infant gull?) As I walk, I think about how or why these birds seem to personify the antipathy many city-dwellers direct towards the natural world, as if gulls transgress by crossing an elusive, invisible boundary between them and us. We seem to have lost the idea of co-existence, if we ever had it. We venerate the concept of wildness without asking what it is. We believe we know what and where is best, purest, wildest and that is invariably, the place furthest from ourselves.

In the mornings of summer, I watch new young birds at the feeders, delving among mealworm and grain. Weeks only from the egg, already they have found their way in the microcosm of biosphere which is my garden. Their lives are so immediate. They hatch, altricial, nidicolous, naked, featherless, blind, dependent and now, so quickly, they're here, flying, negotiating, seeming still so small and young to be out amid the hazards of the world, feeding in the sunshine or in the chill grey of a northern July.

Out of town too, the wide roads are quiet, the stretch of coast beyond the town empty on a warm, late afternoon as I walk and paddle, ankle-deep. The city dog-walkers I usually see here are away, lying on other, hotter beaches. Their dogs will be boarded out in kennels, waiting.

From the beginning of this bay at the edges of the city to the wide sweep north, you can question everything – boundaries, where realms begin or end, what's wild or isn't. Here, there are almost too many lessons in perception, ways of being assailed by words of paradox and contradiction: city or wild, urban or natural, crowded or alone.

On the way home, I stop to see if the owls are still here. For months now I've been watching them in their unlikely golf links home in the shadow of a cluster of high-rise flats. Lightly blown rubbish is strung along perimeter fences, gathered in the hollows of sandy bunkers with their worn plastic rakes. I wait for a while but don't see them. If they are still here, it's probably too late in the day to see them. *Asio flammeus* – short-eared owls – keep strange hours, the hours of nightclub DJs, of wakeful infants.

I came to see them first with a friend, an expert bird-watcher and listener who told me they were here. On an ice-bright morning we watched these open-country, nomadic fliers; all-seeing, all-hearing, wild, flying from the dunes on long, narrow wings like feathered frisbees, turning, landing, staring from dark-ringed yellow eyes from their fence-post perches, unbothered by our watching. Skylarks hopped at our feet as we followed the movement of the low circling, hovering birds, as we took in the angle of their dives before seeing through our lenses the small pouch of fur, the pair of dangling feet, our hearts swopping elation for pity in an instant. Birds flown from other realms, from poetry, the liminal watches of dusk and night – as they flew, myth and omen, human superstition, the patronage of goddesses trailed behind them from snuff and rust and copper feathers.

After I'd seen the owls first, I thought a lot about the place they'd chosen, this not-distant, not obviously wild place and suddenly, it felt undervalued and far too fragile. Who fights for the scruffy, the rubbish blown, edge-of-the-city urban? Who sees it as a rich habitat for anything? Who fights to protect what humans don't see as wild or beautiful or precious to themselves alone? Who knows that everything, in one way or another, can be truly wild?

I walk up the dunes a little way to look over the sea. Against the horizon, the oil vessels which usually rush busily to and from the platforms out at sea, look motionless, fixed, as if they've been abandoned. They seem to fade into a sea filled with luminous evening light, into an eau-de-nil and sea-glass coloured sky. (A couple of miles away, the harbour's crammed with supply vessels no longer fully occupied. Someone told me recently how much it costs a day for them to languish but I can't remember now. A lot, I just remember that.) As I turn away, I think of ghost ships, symbols, parables about folly, wealth, destruction.

SUMMER

The rush hour's muted, the air still unusually warm. There aren't many evenings here when one can sit outside comfortably but on this one, I do. I take a candle to read by as it darkens. Time in summer seems too fast and too slow, an illusion of day-length or light or the novelty of heat. The swifts are shrieking in the evening sky. Bats flick round the corners of the house. This is the moment, they seem to say, this one, now.

Esther Woolfson, 2016

August

Aug. 1.   We destroyed a strong wasp's nest, consisting of many combs: there were young in all gradations, from fresh-laid eggs to young wasps emerging from their aurelia state; many of which came forth after we had kept the combs 'til the next day. Where a martin's nest was broken that contained fledge young: the dams immediately repaired the breach, no doubt with a view to a second brood.

Aug. 5.   Mr Grimm the artist left me. Began to gather apricots. Put out two rows of celeri: the ground dry & harsh.

Aug. 6.   [Meonstoke] Wheat-harvest begun at E. Tisted & West meon.

Aug. 10.   [Selborne] Hay not housed at Meonstoke & Warnford.

Aug. 15.   [Chilgrove] Sun, & clouds, sultry, showers about.

Aug. 16–27.[Ringmer.]

Aug. 20.   Timothy, the tortoise weighs just six pounds three quarters & two ounces & an half: so is encreased in weight, since Aug. 1775, just one ounce and a half.

Aug. 26.   While the cows are feeding in moist low pastures, broods of wagtails, white & grey, run round them close up to their noses, & under their very bellies, availing themselves of the flies, & insects that settle on their legs, & probably finding worms & larvae that are roused by the trampling of their feet. Nature is such an oeconomist, that the most incongruous animals can avail themselves of each other! Interest makes strange friendships.

Aug. 27. [Isfield] Grey, sun, sweet day.

Aug. 28. [Ringmer] The tortoise eats voraciously: is particularly fond of kidney-beans. Vast halo round the moon.

Aug. 29. [Findon] Full moon. The rams begin to pay court to the ewes.

Aug. 30. [Chilgrove] Mr Woods of Chilgrove thinks he improves his flock by turning the east-country poll-rams among his horned ewes. The east-country poll sheep have shorter legs, & finer wool; & black faces, & spotted fore legs; & a tuft of wooll in their fore-heads. Much corn of all sorts still abroad. Was wetted thro' on the naked downs near Parham -ash. Some cuckoos remain. N.B. From Lewes to Brighthelmstone, & thence to Beeding-hill, where the wheat-ear traps are frequent no wheat-ears are to be see: But on the downs west of Beeding, we saw many. A plain proof this, that those traps make a considerable havock among that species of birds.

Aug. 31. [Selborne] Fine harvest day. Some corn housed.

Reverend Gilbert White, The Naturalist's Journal, *1776*

Radiant sunshine illuminates the Parish Church of St Mary and All Saints, Fotheringhay, for centuries a prominent feature of the landscape, reassuring and resplendent, and a summer's-blue sky with only occasional clouds forms the backdrop to its ornate limestone pinnacles and octagonal bell tower.

The churchyard has become an area of species-rich beauty, a peaceful place that provides sanctuary for both flora and fauna. The semi-natural grassland within it contrasts markedly with the arable countryside across the stone wall, stretching out linear to the horizon. There is buzzing activity in here amongst the graves, and signs that life carries on through the seasons. My footsteps on the golden gravel path send several rabbits scattering from their grazing, tails bobbing and with gentle thud of paws, back to the warren that has reportedly been here since medieval times.

Sweeping paths cut through swards of fine, fizzing meadowgrass, creating layers that climb up bright-orange lichen-encrusted headstones. Cocksfoot in tufts is buffered alongside sweet vernal grass, post-solstice breezes tickling the vanilla-scented spikelets. These entangled rhizomes weave beneath every monument, standing, broken or fallen, and are then carpeted by rounded heads of white clover flowers that attract squadrons of bumblebees. Heavily laden and off-balance, they alight on the delicate rosy tints of petals in their quest to harvest nectar.

Ivy can be both a curse and a blessing. Its rambling vines can ruin and cover many headstones, but here, dense growth up a tall Victorian grave marker spills onto a wall, providing a nesting site for a pair of blackbirds – potentially with a second brood by this point in summer – and the skilfully woven cup sits precariously low, at risk from predators. From a vantage spot I can see three chocolate-flecked, greenish-blue eggs; soon returns a keen-eyed female, closely followed by a male chattering an alarm call.

Dappled rays under the crown of an old oak tree create pockets of shading on the uneven ground; fronds of hart's tongue ferns sprout from cracks in moss-cushioned displaced tombs, shifted over time, and are spun with silken spider's thread. Mangled tree roots create damp-smelling hollows where leaf litter collects and woodlice scuttle in the detritus. I spy a robin who has been following me, flying from each weathered cross to coped stone, disappearing into a patch of lime-tinged wood spurge. *Crunch, crunch* goes a pile of mottled garden snail shells underfoot, devoid of occupants and a sign that a thrush has had a tasty meal using the slabs to crack them open. Other visitors to the graveyard noted by mere traces of their presence are foxes. Along the perimeters are pungent scats, twisty reddish-brown hairs caught on wire and a pile of pigeon feathers; they ate well yesterday evening, it seems.

Back towards sun-bathed scythed edges of heady wild flowers that are a nod to the meadows of another age – frothy ivory umbellifers punctuated by purple whorls of self-heal, pink rosettes of dove's-foot cranesbill and yellow studs of creeping buttercup. Long-stalked ox-eye daisy smiles cheerfully against the epitaph 'Peace, perfect peace'. It is a setting that soothes the soul, and in the milder months a perfect spot to sit awhile and just breathe in the serenity. A glance at a patch of earth reveals insects going about their daily round; a long, black-bodied rove beetle battles with a blade of grass, antennae fighting like swords and iridescent wings shielding an exposed abdomen. Crickets stop their chirping at my every rustle and start again as soon as I make myself completely still.

From inside the nave evensong can be heard, all enthusiastic organ-playing and a hymn sung with gusto. But this is no match for one of the tiniest birds of the churchyard, the wren. The corner of my eye catches a quick, dull umber dart into the overgrown elder shrubbery under the light of a heraldic stained-glass window. Suddenly making its presence known, a crow perched atop the lead roof caws, beady eyes moving in all directions, watching and calling. Its shiny, indigo-black feathers outstretched, it rocks forwards beside a gargoyle who looks on mockingly. This is not the only movement above, amongst the grotesques and flying buttresses; for the air is alive with the frenetic humming of wasps swarming around a papery nest, busy producing new queens.

By early evening, with the light dwindling and the few parishioners having left through the ancient wooden lychgate, a twilight spectacle starts in the sky, of swallows soaring, gulping beakfuls of insects whilst performing aerial acrobatics. The sneezing call of a chaffinch erupts from a hawthorn and is echoed by the wheeze of a greenfinch, the slow winding-down of a warm day. Shadows grow longer by each memorial in this resting place and dandelion clocks stream silently into the air like spirits gliding into the sunset.

Samantha Fernley, 2016

Thyme. 1. Wild Thyme *Thymus Serpyllum*, aest. fl. July and August. There are many varieties of the above; it is sometimes called Mother of Thyme. 2. Basil Thyme *Th. Acinos*, aest. fl. July and August. The *Phalaena Papilionaria* lives on wild Thyme, and Bees are so fond of these and other aromatic plants, that it might be worthwhile for the farmer to cultivate them on purpose for them. Virgil praises this sweet herb in his Bucolics.

Thomas Furly Forster, The Pocket Encyclopaedia of Natural Phenomena, *published 1827*

A brown hawker cruises, three feet above the ground, locked in a straight line. Seemingly heading somewhere in a hurry, it's keeping to the speed limit. It is focused on a point ahead, which none of us can see but which is clearly the target.

We're at Brockholes, in Lancashire, where Sophie Leadsom, the former reserve manager, describes this insect as a First World War fighter plane; it is easy to see why. You can almost hear the engine as it moves steadily on, crossing the battlefields of France which, in this instance, are the lakes and meadows of a nature reserve.

The brown hawker is not the only member of the Odonata family at the reserve; dragonflies and damselflies are a major feature of spring and summer. Wander close to any grassy clump and matchsticks of blue, black and red will rise up after a couple of minutes, disturbed by your movement, to bask in the sun. These are damselflies which hold their wings back along their slender bodies when at rest.

Dragonflies are chunkier beasts and bold enough to spread their wings at right angles to their body when they gently land on a leaf along the Brockholes path, or on the banks of a lake or stream.

A total of nineteen species have been recorded here – azure damselfly, banded demoiselle, black darter, black-tailed skimmer, blue-tailed damselfly, broad-bodied chaser, brown hawker, common blue damselfly, common darter, common hawker, emerald damselfly, emperor, four-spotted chaser, large red damselfly, lesser emperor, migrant hawker, red-veined darter, ruddy darter and southern hawker.

This busy family adds splashes of colour to the Brockholes summer and helps to bring the meadows and reed-beds alive with a constant motion on warmer days. Its members are busy providing photo opportunities for lensmen over the water, too. While humans at the Visitor Village immerse themselves in nature, this natural phenomenon flits on around them. As well as providing a great spectacle for visitors, dragonflies and damselflies also serve another purpose: they are very tasty to some predators.

Anyone taking tea and cake in the restaurant at Brockholes will have noticed stunning aerial displays by swallows and sand martins over the Meadow Lake. These birds are amazingly agile, dipping and diving and travelling at high speed before suddenly changing direction and returning to sweep another path over the lake in the hunt for the millions of tiny insects. Look carefully at these birds because you may see something a little different to this hirundine family. The larger birds are, in fact, birds of prey – the sprightly hobbies. Sometimes described as 'over-sized swifts', these elegant small falcons are combing the water for smaller birds and our colourful dragonflies.

The birds nest in the old homes of crows and other birds. These nests tend to be on the edge of a wood so provide good observation points in case of intruders. We have no signs of hobbies nesting at Brockholes yet, but they may already have increased in the woods around the reserve. If so, they will join buzzard and kestrel as residents, despite only renting out a holiday home for summer. Their appearance is great news for the four-year-old reserve, however, and bodes well for hopes that osprey and red kite may, one day, decide to make their nests just off the M6 motorway.

Alan Wright, 2016

Books may be read that tell us of strange forms of life to be found in the deep waters of the great oceans, if we have ships and trawls to help in their quest; but on our own shores we can see for ourselves equally wonderful animals living their lives, which is better than viewing their remains in museums.

When we arrive on almost any shore, even though only of the little harbour where some worn-out boats are drawn up high and dry above high-water, we are soon aware of a brownish-green crab scuttling about on land, peering into corners in search for the garbage on which he feeds. Because he spends most of his time in this way and out of the water, he is known as the Shore-crab or Harbour-crab. In the Tropics there are Landcrabs, that wander far into the interior, and visit the sea only for the purpose of leaving their eggs there. In this country, we have no Land-crabs; but the Shore-crab comes near to earning the title, though he never goes out of sight of the water. He is here of all sizes, up to three or four inches measured across his sharp-toothed upper shell; and his habits enable us to get him into a corner and make ourselves familiar with crab structure, so far as it can be learned from the outside. We see that he is clad in armour, stony if thin, one part forming an almost flat shield which has sloping sides reaching down to the bases of the limbs. There are four pairs of rather flattened, jointed legs with pointed tips, and in front of them a much stouter pair that end in powerful nippers. His eyes are mounted on long stalks, which can be turned upwards so that he can see what is going on behind or to the sides as well as in front. Between the eyes are two pairs of many-jointed feelers which, like those of insects, appear to collect knowledge of what is happening around.

The crab's mouth looks very complicated when he opens the pair of door-like jaws that are jointed and hinged, and discloses other jaws that are shaped like feet. All these play their parts in holding and cutting up the food before it enters the mouth proper, which is quite small. He is a general feeder, but you will find that he has a distinct preference for animal matter.

Looking at the crab from above, its body covered by this shield, we should not be likely to include him among the animals that are built up of rings, as we know the insects are. But if we turn him over on his back, we shall find joint lines across the body and similar lines on the 'tail,' which is really his hind-body tucked closely under him to be out of the way. We shall be able to make out this structure more clearly when we come across some other members of his class that keep their bodies less closely folded.

Very striking along the beach is the line of heaps and rolls of seaweed left by the last high-tide when it turned. Some people turn over these heaps to get from them the finer seaweeds that grow in the deeper water, that have been torn off by the breakers and thrown up by the waves. As a rule, these are bruised and broken by this treatment; but wrapped up in the heap you may often find other things of interest, such as small shells, starfish, jelly-fish and the eggs of cuttle-fish. There: I have used the names of three things ending in 'fish,' and not one of the three is a fish; we must not allow such names to mislead us.

Here are the low rocks, with many hollows cut in their surface and filled with clear water in which we can see many creatures swimming, gliding and walking. We will look into one closely by and by. First, let us enquire into some of the many things that are sticking on the dry parts of the rocks. Their active life is led under water, but between tides they are left in the air, and do not mind it; though there are many others that would be killed quickly by the change. Most plentiful of these rock ornaments are the rough grey patches that cover a great part of the surface, and which are very trying if you have climbed on the rocks with bare feet after a swim. These are Acorn Barnacles; and if you look at them closely you will see that each one of the crowd is a little cone with the top cut off, as it were, and the opening closed by a pair of doors. Whilst out of the water, these doors are kept closed, to prevent the animal within from drying up; but in this little pool adjoining you can see the doors opening and closing at short intervals, and at every opening a fairy plume is thrust out which expands, curls up and retires behind closed doors. That is the way in which the Acorn Barnacle catches its food. You did not see anything caught! That is because it consists of things too minute for us to notice, but it was there all the same; and you may conclude from the abundance of Acorn Barnacles that a good living is made by means of these delicate fishing-nets.

Edward Step, Nature Rambles: An Introduction to Country-lore, *1930*

Forget everything you thought was true about nature. Fairies do exist, but they are small, fluffy and chubby, and fly around, right under our noses, working their magic.

In early spring, fairy queens have just woken up after a long winter hibernating, the warmth of the sun coaxing them out of their slumber. The only thing on their minds is to find nourishment; sleeping for that long makes them very hungry. They feed on the sugary nectar produced by the UK's wild flowers, and this is the best time to witness them busily buzzing around, filling up for the year ahead. It always gives me pleasure to see my first fairy in flight. Their next job is to find a nest, which is important if they are to produce more fairies for next year. Most species make nests in the ground, and they will use ready-made holes whenever possible; their favourite place is an old mouse hole.

We are of course talking about bumblebees. These humble creatures have played a part in folklore ever since humans starting documenting the world around them. They are heavily linked with magic and if one is seen buzzing round your house it is said to mean a visitor is coming. In Celtic folklore bees are seen as beings of great wisdom and messengers between worlds. Bumblebees and fairies have always been linked and, to me, bumblebees are the real fairies of our natural world.

Bumblebees are known by many names; until the Second World War they were called humble bees. Some of you may know the name Dumbledore, which also refers to a bumblebee.

I like to refer to them as 'bumblefairies'. A 'humble bumble' fairy. The word 'bumble' has been perfectly chosen; next time you watch one in flight you will see why they are so called. It means 'to blunder awkwardly, to stumble or stagger' – what a perfect way to describe the beauty of clumsy flight.

Bumblebees are found all over the world but they prefer temperate climates such as ours. Being furry and plump, they can't take too much heat. They cope very well in cooler conditions because they are experts in regulating their body temperature. If you ever see one 'shivering' it is in fact heating itself up in order to fly. After all, it takes a lot of energy to get a chubby little bee off the ground.

Worldwide there are 250 species, all unique in their appearance and behaviour. Each has a different set of coloured bands to help identify it, and they come in a variety of sizes. Here in the UK we have twenty-four species, eight of which can be commonly seen. When we think of a bumblebee, yellow and black stripes come to mind; but there are many more varieties. My personal favourite, the Common Carder, is covered in ginger hair, while the Red-tailed bumblebee is all black with – you guessed it, a red tail. Next time a bee bumbles past, take a closer look; there is more to it than you imagine.

It is still spring and the queen's next job is to lay and rear her first batch of eggs. She sits on the eggs and keeps them warm by 'shivering' her body. She feeds them for a couple of weeks, and by early summer they are fat enough to become adults. These will all be female, and they have a very important job: to look after the colony. Some are cleaner bees, who keep the nest in tip-top condition, while others guard it from intruders. The rest spend their time collecting nectar and pollen from flowers. Warm summer days are when we see the smaller workers flying around. The queen stays in the nest; she is waited on by her worker bees and tells them what to do all season long. It's the females who do all the work in the bumblebee world.

These mystical insects have always been of great interest to me. I first came into contact with them as a child when I used to rescue them from my garden pond. Offering up a concoction of sugar and water on a teaspoon, I would watch their long tongues emerge to feed and wait for them to gain the strength to fly away. But where were they going? Why were they so busy? Little did I know at the time the vital role they were playing in my life.

The importance of these furry wonders has been publicised greatly in recent years, but it seems that we are still not grasping it. That's the thing with magic; it's hard to believe unless you see it happening. Pollination from insects contributes over £400 million to the UK economy every year. Bees pollinate peas, tomatoes, raspberries and strawberries. Imagine a world without these foods; or one where they are very scarce and expensive, which is what would happen without bees pollinating our crops. One solution to this problem is planting more flowers. Agricultural practices have reduced our wildflower meadows and in the last eighty years two species of bumblebee have already become extinct. We must not underestimate the potential of our gardens, which cover one million acres in the UK. It is best to plant bee-friendly flowers, rich in pollen and nectar: foxgloves and lavender are among the bees' favourites.

Late summer is upon us and this is when the males come into the equation. Males exist for the sole purpose of reproduction. They have no sting and don't collect pollen. They really do have a relaxing lifestyle. The rest of the colony has been busy working all summer long. New queens also develop at this time of year, and they leave the nest and mate soon after; the males usually compete in some way to grab a female's attention. Once the new queens have mated they must feed themselves up in order to survive a winter of hibernation. Next spring they will be the queen and create their very own colonies of bumblebees.

It's part of my role for Ulster Wildlife to survey these magical creatures on our nature reserves. This is the best part of my day, when I get to walk around and look for different species, identify them and distinguish between queens, workers and males. I just hope that the buzz of bumbles will fill our countryside for years to come: summer wouldn't be the same without them. I guess that's up to us. The creation of wildflower meadows makes a real difference to these beings. It is easy to see that putting out bird food feeds hungry birds, but the principle is the same – planting wild flowers feeds hungry bees.

Bumblebees and fairies; no wonder they are interlinked in history and folklore, because they are both, after all, guardians of the natural world.

Katy Bell, 2016

Never in all my days did I see a corn harvest like that one. We started swiving, that is reaping, at the beginning of August-month, and we left the stooks standing in the fields till it should be time for the love-carriage, for the weather was so fine that they took no harm. It was the custom, if a farmer hadna much strength about him, that he should fix on a day for the neighbours to come and give a hand in the lugging of the grain. But up to that time, the weather being so good, we worked alone. It was up in the morning early, and no mistake! Such mornings as they were, too, with a strong heady sweetness in the air from the ripened corn, and the sun coming up stately as a swan into the vasty sky that had no cloud. Mother was very peärt and lively, what with the hot weather, which was good for the rheumatics, and the thought of easing-off the work which was to come when the harvest was gotten in. She'd be up and about at five, getting us our breakfast, and then off we'd go, with only just enough of clo'es on to be decent, and with our wooden harvest bottles full of small beer. We always had a brewing for the rep, that is, the reaping. This year we brewed a deal more, for there'd be all the neighbours to find in victuals and drink at the love-carriage. Looking back, it always seems to me that there was a kind of dwelling charm on all that time. Gideon was more contented than I've ever seen him, for there were two things that contented him, namely, to work till he dropped, and to finish what he set out to do. To see all his farm set with these rich stooks, sound and ripe, with never a sign of the weevil nor

of mildew nor the smut, was very life to him. He was all of a
fever to get it safe in stack, but we were bound to wait till the
day fixed. Jancis was to come on that day, to help in the leasing.
And it seemed to me as she ought to go atop of the last load
with blossoms about her, like the image they were used to set
up there, for she seemed a part of the harvest, with all that pink
and gold.

As for me, I went all dazed and dumb with wonder. To think
it was true, 'The Maister be come!' To think as he'd looked at me
and hadna hated me! To think as all that time we spent in the
midst of the painted dragon-flies by the mere was true, as true
as daily bread! When I called to mind the things he'd said, and
still more the things he'd looked, I was like to swound. Dear to
goodness, how I did sing, those early dawns, when the dews lay
heavy after a ketch of frost, and the corn rustled and stirred in
the wind of morning!

When we went out, the leaves of the late-blooming white
clover would be folded tight, and the shepherd's hour-glass shut.
I'd watch them, in the minutes I took for rest, opening soft and
slow like timid hears. Then Mother would come with our noon-
ing, creeping over the fields in her black like a little sad-coloured
bird, and sometimes singing *Barley Bridge* in her old, small
voice, yet was sweet. Then, after the noon-spell, through the
long, blazing evening (for with us all the time after noon is
called evening) I'd watch the shepherd's hour-glass shutting up
again, and the white clover leaves, folding as the dews came. We
took turns to go whome and milk, then we'd have our tea in the
field, and at it again. All the while I thought of Kester, as would
soon be working at the coloured weaving in the great city. But
when my heart said he was working for me as well as hisself, I

hushed it, saying that it was but his flaming look that made me think it, for he hadna said it, and so it was only that the wish fathered the thought. But I did dream of the fifty pounds I was to have, a great fortune, it seemed. And I did plan how I'd get to be cured as quick as might be, so when Kester came back after his time away I'd stand afore him with as proper a face as even Felena, though I hoped not so forrard. [...]

It was very early when the waggons began to roll into the fold, with a solemn gladsome sound, and each with its own pair of horses or oxen. Each farmer brought his own men and his own waggon, and sometimes he brought two. The teams were decked out with ribbons and flowers, and some had a motto as well, such as, 'Luck to our Day', or 'God bless the Corn'. It was a fine thing to see the big horses, with great manes on their fetlocks, groomed till they shone like satin, stepping along as proud as Lucifer, knowing very well how long the waggoner had been, a-plaiting their ribbons. The oxen were good to see, also, for their horns were all bedecked, and about their necks were thick chains of Sweet William and Travellers' Joy and corn. Miller came among the first, with his gig and the old coach horse, the best he had, poor man. And very good work they did, too, for it's surprising what a deal you can get onto a gig if you put a set of wings on top.

It was time for me to go and give the folks welcome, so I got Miller's Tim to mind the trestles, and left him with a big meat patty, sitting at the top of one of the tables, with half the patty in one cheek, ready to drive away birds and cats and dogs, and even goblins out of fairyland, after the patty.

Mary Webb, Precious Bane, *1924*

Threshing Day

Then came August, I recall, and
Bromley Wood, a snuggled hamlet
dozed in the stifling warm.

By faraway Birchwood a bird-scarer
rent the languid teatime hum
with a brusque report

and nearer, the indignant crow
patrolled the mossy cottage roof
excavating grubs with a twig.

On the verge, idle now, stood
the old threshing machine
blanched from livid scarlet

to dusty, peeling pink
the steady meter of rod, shaft
and crank, dwindled to silence

now home to the swift
gathering sustenance, force
for the looming southward hegira.

Rain arrived in fat, fragrant
smudges, which the beaten earth
absorbed like blotting paper

a sudden interjection
a jerk of the shoulder
prompting the question . . .

What would the threshers say
their brawny arms etched by straw
backs bent under the heavy stook

like so much tribute at Ceres' altar
long-since dispersed like chaff
on a century of summer breezes?

What would they think of us today
this threshing day? Do they know
the thing we have become?

Julian Beach, 2016

High summer on the North Wessex Downs and the wheat field crackles and pops like a bowl of cereal as it ripens under the sun.

The down's broad flank is in full sun and we seek the refuge of a small hawthorn, flopping down on the chalk grassland among the high, pylon whine of grasshoppers, hoverflies and bees. The short, springy turf is a riot of rich and fragrant colour.

Here are clustered bellflower, centaury and hawkbits, fine fairy flax, chalk milkwort and orchids, the delightfully named squinancywort and scabious, blue as Wedgwood china. Cinnabar moths flash flamenco skirt-wings of charcoal and scarlet and marbled white butterflies skip by like slivers of marbled icing. Here too is the heady, kitchen-garden scent of wild thyme and basil, marjoram and salad burnet. This close mat of tough plant life is best experienced at eye level, lying down so you can feel the hard curve of the hill beneath, the thinness of its layer of grass and soil, where it is also easy to press your face into the earth and breathe in an old ocean's worth of summers, the sun's stored heat emanating from it.

We head uphill again, pausing for breath to watch a hovering kestrel, pinned to the poster-blue sky by its eye. Below is a panorama of harvest in progress. The barley fields ripple like the pelt of a moving animal in the stiff, warm breeze. Great long-shadowed straw megaliths stand in already harvested fields, whilst others are scored by thick tramlines of straw waiting to be baled. The country is a golden parquet floor.

In the afternoon, the combine turns into the field behind the house with an excitable roar. We watch from the garden gate as it greedily gathers the crop to its blades; a gobbling monster fanning dusty chaff like a desert storm. We wait to see what flees from it. Rabbits, from all directions. And, as the machine turns for the last stand of crop, a young fox canters off towards the wood, glancing back disdainfully over its shoulder at a rude awakening.

The young buzzards that keep up a day-long mewing to their parents descend on other, suddenly easy prey. One carries off a grass snake, which dangles limply like a length of rope, while its sibling tackles a rat, in situ.

We let a respectable amount of time pass after the machinery leaves the field – and then the fun begins. First, we are out on the edges of the long golden windrows, furtively filling sacks with armfuls of straw for the animals. A neighbour across the field is doing the same – a sort of modern gleaning for us Estate cottagers. It is a small, insignificant amount, but it feels naughty all the same.

And then we run: leaping the heaped, orderly rows in a steeplechase, the dog flying ahead of us. I have done this for almost every year of my life – and so have our children. It's a sort of personal harvest celebration. We return to pat any incursions back into shape and, breathlessly laughing, leave the field. The field-edge shadows are already breeding tawny owls.

After dark we go 'lamping' for wildlife in the Landrover, specifically for the owls that drift in to take advantage of suddenly bald, exposed, vole-rich prairies. Gold dust hangs in the air.

We drive slowly with an eye on the fence line that divides the stubble from the downland and the careful, measured sweep of a million-candle bulb in careful hands. Almost immediately we spot our first barn owl. Poised on a post, it turns its heart-shaped face to us, huge, black, light-gathering eyes unfathomable dew-ponds either side the feather covered beak. It bobs its attention between us and the ground, its white chest a subtle contrast to its lightly toasted, warm apricot back, feathery hocks meeting above turned out toes.

We leave it hunting, only to come across another, quartering the stubble in wavering, moth-like flight, rowing steadily through the lamp's beam. Its big convex face is tilted like a satellite dish to the ground, listening hard for the squeaks, squabbles, rustles and reorganisations of small, suddenly exposed animals. It glows in the lamp's light, ignoring us, a halo of barley dust glittering around it.

In our second field, the sweep of the big lamp takes in the furthest of the loaded trailers. There is a pair of tawny owls on opposing corners. They are like bedknobs above a mattress big enough to conceal a dried pea to test a princess.

All the while, distant and close the combines roar into the night with the sound of a billion bees, the big swing of lights as they round the night headlands, a facsimile of the sunlit glint of horse brasses on the turn of a hardworked furrow.

Our last owl of the night is our third barn owl. Right on the far side of this 2,000-acre estate, it foots a freshly caught rat on a fence post, affording us the merest glance before bracing to pull and stretch its meal to the full height of its body. The owl's balance is compromised with the effort and as it rocks back on rear claws that grip the wooden post, its hairy toes digging further into its prey for purchase. We are just metres away.

This bird's feathers are wheatfield gold, dappled grey and spotted, as if the pin in the wing were still visible. Its beak and feet glisten darkly with what is probably blood. Before we leave it to its meal, it throws back its head to gollop down a chunk.

In the morning, the bales are tractored off the field behind the house. Even though I know the plough will go in before long, I hope for winter stubble and its attendant wildlife. The season begins, subtly, to change. The light is more nuanced, the days quieter, fresher and, in this landlocked county, the breeze somehow has the salt, ozone tang of the sea in it.

Nicola Chester, 2016

High Summer

I never wholly feel that summer is high,
However green the trees, or loud the birds,
However movelessly eye-winking herds
Stand in field ponds, or under large trees lie,
Till I do climb all cultured pastures by,
That hedged by hedgerows studiously fretted trim,
Smile like a lady's face with lace laced prim,
And on some moor or hill that seeks the sky
Lonely and nakedly, – utterly lie down,
And feel the sunshine throbbing on body and limb,
My drowsy brain in pleasant drunkenness swim,
Each rising thought sink back and dreamily drown,
Smiles creep o'er my face, and smother my lips, and cloy,
Each muscle sink to itself, and separately enjoy.

Ebenezer Jones, published 1843

In July and August, the fields and hills often seem hushed – almost arid – in the heat. Greenness turns parched or brown and only the yellow-hammer twitters in the hot afternoon. But by the river there is no such stillness. This is the river's bountiful, luxuriant time. Along the banks, great clumps of flowering plants spring up and bloom like a herbaceous border – purple loosestrife, the yellow daisies of the fleabane, fluffy, pink, hemp agrimony, great willow herb, the huge white whorls of the great water dock, and dark-red, tough, square-stemmed figworth (which is pollinated almost only by wasps). They make fine cover for the fisherman to stalk a rising trout. In the water itself – in the stiller reaches – other, fantastic plants are in bloom: the yellow water lily, its long stalks trailing deep – sometimes several feet to the bed of the river. This is the lily called 'brandy-bottle', from the shape of the big, green seed-pod when the flower is over. Close by there may be arrowhead (so-called from the shape of the leaves rising clear out of the water), with its white, purple-eyed flowers branching out of the main stalk in little clusters. The flowering rush likes still water, and here it puts up its head of frail, deep-pink blooms (three big petals alternating with three small ones) on a stalk which is often as much as three feet tall. The crowfoots (or crowfeet?), of which there are many, are water buttercups, though their flowers are white and their leaves submerged; and the hornwort and mare's tail (which are more likely to be found in canals, perhaps, than in rivers) have a strangely old, prehistoric look, as though they once grew in dinosaurs' swamps long ago.

Unexpected things may happen by a river in time of drought. One hot August afternoon, many years ago, a certain fisherman was working conscientiously through the inactive time of the day. (Trout rise best at morning and evening.) Coming to a wide bed of tall reeds, he saw that some fairly big animal was moving in there; and a moment later a badger, whom the heat must have driven down to drink in broad daylight, pushed its way out and lumbered off up the slope to the near-by woods. Another day that same fisherman, working up a side-stream, came upon a swimming otter, which pulled itself out and bounded away, with a lithe leaping, across the water-meadow.

During the earlier part of the summer, the heron is a hard worker, and as long as he is undisturbed will often stab and paddle away in the running shallows for hours, coming and going to his nestlings with slow, heavy beats of his grey wings. In contract is the dashing speed of the swifts and swallows, which seem to fill the whole river with movement as they turn and flash, hunting fliers over the water; or break the surface for an instant (either sipping, or snatching a floating fly) before racing up and away. In the sedge hover the great dragonflies (four-engined dragonflies, we used to call them), green, and ochre, and glittering blue, with their great, panelled eyes and segmented bodies. Like hummingbirds, they hold themselves poised in the air, vanish as they dart away in a split second and then resume their tense stillness a few yards along the bank. In a shallow pool under the bank a great pike, two feet long, basks and dozes in the warm water. The water-mint has a sleepy smell; but if we are asleep, it is a sleep like Caliban's. When we wake, we cry to dream again.

Richard Adams, Nature Through the Seasons, *1975*

I n the hottest and brightest season of the year, few think to turn to the darkest hours for their wildlife thrills. But there are those among us who welcome the night gladly, for it brings hidden delights. During the hours when humans sleep there are moths to be found. And whereas moths can be found during the day, even in winter, it is summer nights that give the best variety and spectacle.

It's a labour of love, hauling the box out of the shed or from under the table, trying not to trip over the cables, debating where the best spot is to set it up, and worrying whether the neighbours will mind the glow. Getting it into position, we glance at the sky to see how long it will be before the daylight fades. When waiting for night to fall, a summer's day can drag on terribly.

At last the sun has decided to sink and the day is drawing to an end. With a gleeful rubbing of hands and a final check that everything is in place, we plug in the cable and switch on. The garden again comes alive as the light of the trap spreads out into the neighbourhood. There's a choice of lamps. Some prefer the soft blue that casts a magical spell across the flowers and hedgerow so that you almost expect delicate fairies to be flitting here and there. Others use the poetic sounding mercury vapour bulbs, whose light is stronger and more forceful, a brilliant white that is too bright to look at directly.

Morning dawns, the eastern horizon showing a pink bloom that spreads across the sky like a blush on a fair cheek. Oranges and yellows appear as well, until the sky settles into a lovely blue that promises a wonderfully sunny day ahead. Already we have been at the trap, rising from our beds with both eagerness and a touch of trepidation. What will be found in the garden, drawn to the light shining among the shadows.

Before the trap itself, we need to inspect the surrounding grass, its green stems hiding the first moth. Care is required. It wouldn't do to step on anything. But at the same time, we're excited and want to hurry. And there, clinging with its six legs to a grass steam, the first moth of the morning. No matter the species, it is always a thrilling and humbling experience.

Underestimated by many, moths are often forgotten. This must be set straight. Whilst butterflies are regarded as beautiful, moths are usually mocked, called 'drab and boring'. Not so. Take the garden tiger moth, with its striking brown and white upper wings and, if lucky, you'll see a glimpse of its hind wings which flash in a startling display of red and blue: a summer beauty if ever there was one. The other tigers are similarly resplendent in their contrasting colours and always brighten a moth trap. By day, their disruptive camouflage hides them from sight just like that of their namesakes in hot, distant jungles.

Continuing this theme of striking colours, an elephant hawk-moth will always fit the bill. Bright pink and green, it is the perfect antidote to the stereotypical brown ascribed to moths. As its wings vibrate and slowly warm in the morning sun, like a plane revving for takeoff, you feel a sense of wonder at this incredible sight.

It would be an omission not to mention the more subtle, yet astonishing patterns of yet more species: the buff-tip's extraordinary twig-like camouflage; the metallic glow of the burnished brass and bold spot; and the intricate designs of the black arches and puss moth.

Of course, there are plenty of vivid moths to discover, but there are many who are rather more modest in their attire. Large yellow underwings are a common sight, seeming to take up all the available room and becoming the bane of many moth traps. They are worthy of praise even so, their humble overcoat concealing vivid yellow petticoats, which are revealed as they fly away.

It is easy to be fascinated by every species, through their colouration, shape or patterning. Even the names of many are poetic – lilac beauty, peach blossom, frosted orange, Kentish glory, true lover's knot and fiery clearwing. Just reading their names stirs a sense of mystery and anticipation.

As the trap is slowly emptied, every moth's identity is puzzled out and noted down as a record, to be sent off to join the vast archive of data. But in that moment, the data feels less important. Kneeling by the trap, there is delight as each one is plucked out of the depths and brought into the morning light. The moths try to make sense of the situation, their antennae quivering gently in time with the heartbeats of those looking at them. There is a brief sense of connection, despite the great differences between human and moth, until the moth takes flight. While some of its brethren skim beneath the sun, it will head for dark nooks and crannies, to hide away from the dangers of the day.

Megan Shersby, 2016

Sparrows *Fringilla domestica*. Sparrows congregate in August and September, and it is then that they feed in flocks in the standing corn, and are mistakenly destroyed for the mischief they do. Intelligent farmers are, however, now beginning to be aware that these, as well as most birds, do more good by the vermin they destroy in spring and summer than they do mischief by the grain and fruit they eat in autumn.

Thomas Furly Forster, The Pocket Encyclopaedia of Natural Phenomena, *published 1827*

A voice of summer

In this one of all fields I know the best
All day and night, hoarse and melodious, sounded
A creeping corncrake, coloured like the ground,
Till the cats got him and gave the rough air rest.

Mechanical August, dowdy in the reeds,
He ground his quern and the round minutes sifted
Away in the powdery light. He would never lift
His beady periscope over the dusty hayseeds.

Cunning low-runner, tobogganing on his breast
He slid from sight once, from my feet. He only
Became the grass; then stone scraped harsh on stone,
Boxing the compass round his trivial nest.

– Summer is now diminished, is less by him.
Something that it could say cannot be spoken –
As though the language of a subtle folk
Had lost a word that had no synonym.

Norman MacCaig, 1962

Distant combines mutter across the fields, efficient yellow monsters biting down the corn. The harvest itself is a shifting dust cloud which forbids approach. Gone for good is the communal toil and the communal relief and joy which naturally succeeded it. Other than the farmer and his couple of men, no one any longer feels a thing about harvest, if the truth were told. Some old hymns and decorations a few weeks hence will do their best to resurrect some of the old emotion. And then no aching arms and backs in the pews – unless one happens to have been ringing the bells. Never again that hard corporate way of experiencing what, still within living memory, had been the common fate of any village, which was at this time to be made to work all hours so as to have bread.

For the best part of a fortnight the temperature has made the heatwave mark, thus making the grade in classic English-summer terms. Blue dawns, blue dusks, and in between a scorcher. 'How do you like this?' we say in passing, instead of Good morning. 'Chalk it up,' we say, 'a summer at last!' The horizon wavers and such creatures as stand in meadows pant gratefully in one another's shadows. Not so mankind. For us a proper summer demands appropriate events and these, unlike harvests, are far from being left to a handful of participants. Thus through the August lanes we meander through the hot Saturday afternoon to Little Tey, where I am to open the church fête in the rectory garden. Accompanying us is Joachim from Berlin. It is his first fête and, although none of us know it as yet, following it will be his first cricket match. At two o'clock sharp Lady Laurie takes me to a familiar looking prop left over from the open-air performance of *Romeo and Juliet* a few days ago, the balcony no less, and at once I give sincere voice to the glories of the English fête which, even were it pouring cats and dogs, is never called off, never any different, indeed always gaining when in adversity. But to have a fête on a day like this, well what could be more perfect! Who could ask for more? Joachim, as yet innocent of fête drill and with a charitable amount of money burning a hole in his pocket, is pointed towards the cake stall. An unseemly rush to the cake stall always follows the morning speech, we advise him. Whereas, at a cricket match, whether on a burning or a freezing wicket, rush is not a word which applies.

We come across this idyll unexpectedly and even hardened rustics such as Ian and myself are momentarily stunned by the perfection which stretches before us. We meant no more than to show Joachim the wall-paintings in Copford church but our way is blocked by the kind of unconsciously formed master-piece which all comes together when a heatwave wills it. Living figures almost still in their whites on a living green, a long lime avenue coolly leading to a great house and in the churchyard the grave of Eric Ravilious, a fine artist killed in 1942.

Ronald Blythe, Out of the Valley: Another Year at Wormingford, *2007*

In an August Garden

Where, I asked, did the spiders come
suspended huge and still,
as skies cooled and the dews grew long,
backs printed with a skull?
Where were they when sun burned my crown,
I slashed the browning roses down?
I dare not lean through borders lest
I spin them out through homeless air
unlink their glistening nets.

This year, I saw. Crumpled and gold
crammed in a fold of leaf
small spiders swarmed across my hands,
spilled to the ground underneath.
Then came the first web, braving rain,
the centred spider, one brown grain.
So spiders do not come. They grow.
Wind shivers worn skin. Now I know,
I must ask where the spiders go.

Alison Brackenbury, 2013

How easy, in the electric light inside the cottage, with the windows so small, to forget the distance to the next house. Actually, no other buildings are visible from this one, and fields separate us from the one or two that are possibly somewhere near. Some shock in stepping outside the door, into the size of it. And surprise because – there is no wind at all. Clear night blue, some stars, a burst of crows cawing and moving out off the mountain, a bat or two, high or low, and an owl, very loud and close. Hard silhouette of the mountain. Small flies tickle. A drop falls in the water butt, which is now full. Small, pink clouds have left the sky to roll in the lap of Cader Idris. Stillness gets inside the holly. Here we are under the open Milky Way, under Vega, with the complete show, the Plough and Cassiopeia resting on the rim of our bowl, and one of the Perseids whipping silently to extinction towards the south east.

Pure postcard on Tuesday. Puffs of cloud overland, and thin cirrus over the sea. Hot enough in the wind to redden us all on Harlech beach. Into the dunes there, barefoot and careful for glass and harsh marram. A sudden glaucous blue patch, like litter, but it is cool sea-holly, tough and heavy. Rest harrow everywhere. Carline thistles, intricate, with glossy white-gold rays. Hollows floored with creeping willow, with catkins, and knotted pearlwort. The mashed urchin cases, chalky, broken, papery, in middens at the waterline. The leathery horseshoe prints, which are the eggs of the necklace shell, sunk in gleaming sand. A damp apple core, shoved into dry sand, with suggestions of sand in the teeth, grit in saliva, cut tongues, spit not thick enough. A crow opens and lifts off with a tilt from the wrack. Crab bits. Pin eyes. White legs. Closed claws. Flies whirl up and land on wrists, with offensive feet. Is there a smell of fish? Yet, also, there is a sudden sweetness in the air, or detected on the fingers. As you come out, the sea warms the back of your calves. Soft, ropey weed wraps your knees. There is the immaculately displayed beach and hills, the picked out houses, grey and white, the neat, complete, strong charcoal grey castle on its diagonally layered rock, where Bran the Blessed feasted for seven years as a decapitated head, while the birds of Rhiannon sang, far out to sea, yet close in the ear, and no song was more beautiful than that, since it came from the other world, the paradise over the water, and could bring back the dead. Heavy water on me, as I stand out, up to the neck, compared to that. The sudden slap and rush over my head from behind, of a swell I did not antic-ipate. Chance and inadequacy. And the hundreds of people, to the right, along the beach. Completely a matter of no dream or final joy. Burnt skin. Greasy pink. Elastic and horny soles. Rubber shoes. A fat youth smacking a girl's legs with a yellow, plastic spade. Folding chairs in hands. Calves full of knotted veins. Loud voices which blemish the rush of water, and love be-tween pieces of sandy meat. No repercussions out of the final air. Not so much a million, unseen relationships, as just a handful of responses. The ridges of the sand unexpectedly hard, banging the foot. The best mountains ringing us, reduced to glamour. Time should be a swift collection of light, clear empty glasses on a biscuit coloured shelf. The scent of the contents detached, adrift, somewhere a little way off, into which one might stumble, but it would be impossible to hold on or understand. Imagine the beach empty. The castle manned. The reduplicated houses gone. The empty shell of an urchin. Little, wafery skulls, which thought would darken and melt. Empty sockets, tilted to every corner of the sky. A sore neck touched by a ruggy shirt collar. Sticky hair. The breaks in sentences longer, this year. The eyes glazed in mid remark. The names vanish, and there is a yawn in the voice. What can string all this together?

August 1982

R. F. Langley, Journals, *published 2006*

I walk, brooding, through buttery sunshine that's heavy in the air. A light wind clatters through the parched leaves of the trees, a shiver that seems to promise relief from the heat but which ultimately just fidgets and idles, toying with the lifeless air. Everything is wilting, fading.

My city-pale skin is already reddening from the exposure, tight and sore – but I hardly notice, distracted by the gorse prickling my elbows. The golden bushes look bright and inviting, but their treacherous flowers conceal thorny branches that threaten unsuspecting walkers. This route will almost certainly cause further grazes, but the only other path to the creek would mean wading through swathes of stinging nettles, so I plough resignedly onwards through the gorse.

As the wind picks up, the rattle of the leaves whisks my thoughts back to the train shuddering out of Liverpool Street and through the baked, gritted-grey London suburbs towards Essex, East Anglia's gentle roll-and-tumble before the flat spread of the Fenlands. For a moment I see myself rumbling towards the salt air, the spatter of mudflats dirtying and dissolving the coastline, and the under-appreciated, sun-bleached fields of wheat and barley.

This walk is the source of many childhood memories, a route patrolled by vigilant dog-walkers which takes you past the burnt-out ruins of an old church, up and over the hills and eventually down through green woods to the river. I skitter down the hill and away from the gorse, my feet automatically finding the right path. Rabbit warrens lace the hill to my left, felted by dandelions gone to seed, reminding me of the stories my mother would tell about the fairies who lived there. I pass a wide oak tree, drift-wood hammered into its side to form a crude ladder. This doesn't make the tree much easier to climb, as I well know, but the hollow in its branches is worth the undignified scramble, with space enough for two friends to perch comfortably at the top.

Crossing a stream almost completely hidden by swollen undergrowth, I pause to admire the few late poppies that are still preening on its banks. Smaller flowers are blooming too, tiny speckles of blue and white and yellow. Trefoil and brooklime and clover, harebell and catsear. Running through the names is comforting; it makes me feel at home here, anchored in this sunny patch of Essex. I drift on, past the fishing lakes, across the chalky road used only by lorries carrying gravel from the pits – and then I pause again, baffled and awestruck.

Before me lies a field of sunflowers, more than I have ever seen in one place. There are hundreds of them crowded there. This field has always been empty before.

The flowers have already started to wither, their perfect Fibonacci spirals crumbling away, but in the late-summer light they have taken on the season's reddish glow, now flaunting autumnal shades of red: amber and sienna and terracotta. The impression is of a sheet of rusting metal, or an evening sun hung low over water. They look as if they are blushing – embarrassed, perhaps, that they are beginning to show their old age. I struggle to absorb it all – the colours, the light, the scale. More than anything, I'm conscious of the serendipity of this moment; I have arrived at exactly the right time to see the sunflowers just before they fade away.

Rhiannon Bull, 2016

Wasps.—Abundance of wasps are said to denote a good fruit year. We have remarked also the converse of this, for in the present season, 1824, perhaps the worst for apples and stone fruit that we remember, there is scarcely a wasp to be seen. In general towards the close of summer they are very numerous, particularly in the month of September. In 1821 they were prodigiously plentiful, and in 1822 there were a great many of them, while 1824 scarcely presented a solitary wasp even where they usually abound.

Thomas Furly Forster, The Pocket Encyclopaedia of Natural Phenomena, *published 1827*

Now the rosy- (and lazy-) fingered Aurora, issuing from her saffron house, calls up the moist vapours to surround her, and goes veiled with them as long as she can; till Phoebus, coming forth in his power, looks everything out of the sky, and holds sharp, uninterrupted empire from his throne of beams. Now the mower begins to make his sweeping cuts more slowly, and resorts oftener to the beer. Now the carter sleeps a-top of his load of hay, or plods with double slouch of shoulder, looking out with eyes winking under his shading hat, and with a hitch upward of one side of his mouth. Now the little girl at her grand-mother's cottage-door watches the coaches that go by, with her hand held up over her sunny forehead. Now labourers look well resting in their white shirts at the doors of rural ale-houses. Now an elm is fine there, with a seat under it; and horses drink out of the trough, stretching their yearning necks with loosened collars; and the traveller calls for his glass of ale, having been with-out one for more than ten minutes; and his horse stands wincing at the flies, giving sharp shivers of his skin, and moving to and fro his ineffectual docked tail; and now Miss Betty Wilson, the host's daughter, comes streaming forth in a flowered gown and ear-rings, carrying with four of her beautiful fingers the foaming glass, for which, after the traveller has drank it, she receives with an indifferent eye, looking another way, the lawful twopence. Now grasshoppers 'fry,' as Dryden says. Now cattle stand in water, and ducks are envied. Now boots, and shoes, and trees by the road side, are thick with dust; and dogs, rolling in it, after issuing out of the water, into which they have been thrown to fetch sticks, come scattering horror among the legs of the spectators. Now a fellow who finds he has three miles further to go in a pair of tight shoes is in a pretty situation. Now rooms with the sun upon them become intolerable; and the apothecary's apprentice, with a bitterness beyond aloes, thinks of the pond he used to bathe in at school. Now men with powdered heads (especially if thick) envy those that are unpowdered, and stop to wipe them up hill, with countenances that seem to expostulate with destiny. Now boys assemble round the village pump with a ladle to it, and delight to make a forbidden splash and get wet through the shoes. Now also they make suckers of leather, and bathe all day long in rivers and ponds, and make mighty fishings for 'tittle-bats.' Now the bee, as he hums along, seems to be talking heavily of the heat. Now doors and brick-walls are burning to the hand; and a walled lane, with dust and broken bottles in it, near a brick-field, is a thing not to be thought of. Now a green lane, on the contrary, thick-set with hedgerow elms, and having the noise of a brook 'rumbling in pebble-stone,' is one of the pleasantest things in the world.

Now, in town, gossips talk more than ever to one another, in rooms, in door-ways, and out of window, always beginning the conversation with saying that the heat is overpowering. Now blinds are let down, and doors thrown open, and flannel waistcoats left off, and cold meat preferred to hot, and wonder expressed why tea continues so refreshing, and people delight to sliver lettuces into bowls, and apprentices water door-ways with tin-canisters that lay several atoms of dust. Now the water-cart, jumbling along the middle of the street, and jolting the showers out of its box of water, really does something. Now fruiterers' shops and dairies look pleasant, and ices are the only things to those who can get them. Now ladies loiter in baths; and people make presents of flowers; and wine is put into ice; and the after-dinner lounger recreates his head with applications of perfumed water out of long-necked bottles. Now the lounger, who cannot resist riding his new horse, feels his boots burn him. Now buck-skins are not the lawn of Cos.* Now jockies, walking in great-coats to lose flesh, curse inwardly. Now five fat people in a stage-coach hate the sixth fat one who is coming in, and think he has no right to be so large. Now clerks in office do nothing but drink soda-water and spruce-beer, and read the newspaper. Now the old clothesman drops his solitary cry more deeply into the areas on the hot and forsaken side of the street; and bakers look vicious; and cooks are aggravated: and the steam of a tavern-kitchen catches hold of us like the breath of Tartarus. Now delicate skins are beset with gnats: and boys make their sleeping companion start up, with playing a burning-glass on his hand; and blacksmiths are super-carbonated; and cobblers in their stalls almost feel a wish to be transplanted; and butter is too easy to spread; and the dragoons wonder whether the Romans liked their helmets; and old ladies, with their lappets unpinned, walk along in a state of dilapidation; and the servant maids are afraid they look vulgarly hot; and the author, who has a plate of strawberries brought him, finds that he has come to the end of his writing.

Leigh Hunt, 'A "Now": Descriptive of a Hot Day', 1820

Author Biographies

Nick Acheson grew up in wellies, watching bog bush-crickets in North Norfolk. A year spent in the Camargue during his degree inspired him to seek wilder landscapes and for ten glorious years he lived in Bolivia. Since returning to the UK he has worked the world over, from Arctic tundras to the Antarctic. He proudly works closely with Norfolk Wildlife Trust, for whom he regularly features in local press and media.

Richard Adams is most famous as the author of *Watership Down*, as well as many other international bestsellers, most of which reflect his fascination with and love for nature. He served in the British Army in World War II and afterwards worked in the Civil Service. He lives in Hampshire.

Kenneth Allsop (d. 1973) was a presenter of current affairs programmes, most famously BBC's *Tonight* programme, in the 1960s and early 1970s. He wrote many novels and short stories which explored his love of birds and the natural world, and was a tireless conservationist, playing a crucial role in saving two hundred acres of ancient woodland in Dorset from being felled for oil drilling.

Jacqueline Bain lives in Paisley, Scotland. She is a former nurse, unable to work due to extensive knee surgery. She enjoys writing fiction and non-fiction in which nature will always feature somewhere. Her main hobbies include bird watching and creating space and homes in the garden for mini-beasts, in between throwing a ball for Bonny, her fourteen-year-old Border collie.

W. N. P. Barbellion was the pseudonym under which Bruce Frederick Cummings (d. 1919) published *The Diary of a Disappointed Man* after discovering he was suffering from multiple sclerosis and only had a short time to live. Described as one of the most moving diaries ever written, it recorded his reflections on nature and on both the brevity and the beauty of life.

Simon Barnes writes about the wild world. He contributes a weekly column to the *Sunday Times Magazine* and his latest book is *The Sacred Combe: A Search for Humanity's Heartland*. He lives in Norfolk with his family and a horse or two.

Julian Beach, originally from Staffordshire and now living in Laugharne, Wales, recently returned to writing after a two-decade estrangement from the muse. He is currently applying the finishing touches to 'The Needwood Poems', inspired by memories of growing up in the ancient Needwood Forest, most of which fell to the encloser's axe in the nineteenth century. He blogs at: julianbeachwriting. wordpress.com.

Katy Bell always wanted to work with wildlife in some form; it has fascinated her ever since she was young. This led her to study Zoology at the University of Edinburgh followed by a Master's in Conservation Biology. She has worked on research projects around the world but always loves coming home to our own special wildlife. She now works for Ulster Wildlife in Northern Ireland.

Kate Blincoe is a nature-loving mother of two and freelance writer for publications such as the *Guardian*. She is the author of *The No-Nonsense Guide to Green Parenting* and is never happier than when exploring the countryside with her family.

Ronald Blythe is the author of more than twenty books, most famously *Akenfield: Portrait of an English Village* (1969), a fictionalised account of a Suffolk village from 1890 to 1966, which became the record of ways of rural life that were rapidly vanishing from Britain. He is also the author of the much-loved and long running 'Words from Wormingford' column in the *Church Times.*

Alison Brackenbury is the author of seven collections of poetry for which she has been the recipient of several awards. Born in Lincolnshire, she was educated at Oxford and now lives in Gloucestershire.

Dawn Bradley has, for the past thirty years, almost always found a home on one side of the Tamar or the other. She grew up in Cornwall and currently resides in Plymouth, where she attended university. The natural world is her greatest source of creative inspiration, whether raising awareness through citizen journalism, painting or simply studying the wildlife spectacles around her.

Nicholas Breton (d. 1626) was a prolific writer of religious and pastoral poems, satires and prose works. Little concrete detail is known about his life, but he was well regarded as an author in his lifetime, although forgotten quickly afterwards. His final book *Fantastickes* (1626), offers great insight into the customs of the era.

Rhiannon Bull has studied at Durham University and the University of Essex, where she is currently working towards an MA in Wild Writing. She is interested in using the written and visual arts to portray the relationship between people and place, exploring the landscape, memories, languages and mythologies that form these relationships.

Jo Cartmell is a lifelong naturalist with a special interest in water voles and wild-flower meadows. She runs the Twitter accounts @WaterVole and @NearbyWild and also blogs for nearbywild.org.uk about her local wildlife.

Nicola Chester writes about the wildlife she finds wherever she is, mostly roaming the North Wessex Downs where she lives with her husband and three children. She has written professionally for over a decade. Nicola is particularly passionate about engaging people with nature and how language can communicate the thrill of wild experiences. You can read her blog here: nicolachester.wordpress.com.

Mark Cocker is a naturalist and the author of ten books about nature, as well has having written on the topic for most national broadsheets, including the *Guardian's* 'Country Diary' column since 1988. For the last three decades he has been dedicated to the restoration of a fen called Blackwater where he lives in Norfolk, and his latest book is *Claxton: Field Notes from a Small Planet.*

James Common is a dedicated naturalist, birder, writer and graduate conservation scientist from Northumberland. He is passionate about all aspects of natural history though his greatest interests lie in the realms of biological recording, ecology and ornithology. Elsewhere James is a keen blogger (commonbynature. co.uk) and a member of A Focus on Nature, the youth nature network.

Charles Dickens (d. 1870) is one of Britain's most famous known and best-loved novelists. Besides establishing, editing and writing for two weekly publications, *Household Words* (1850–9) and *All The Year Round* (1859–1870) and campaigning tirelessly for social justice and reform, he also wrote fourteen novels, including *Oliver Twist* (1837–9), *A Tale of Two Cities* (1859) and *Great Expectations* (1861).

George Eliot was the pseudonym of Mary Ann Evans (d. 1880), a Victorian novelist whose *Middlemarch* (1871–2) was recently voted the greatest British novel of all time by a BBC poll of world critics and academics. Her other major works include *Adam Bede* (1859), *The Mill on the Floss* (1860) and *Silas Marner* (1861).

Paul Evans is a poet, author, broadcaster university lecturer and regular contributor to the *Guardian's* 'Country Diary'. He contributes regularly to many publications, including BBC *Wildlife* and *Country Living*, and is most recently author of *Field Notes from the Edge: Journeys Through Britain's Secret Wilderness*. He lives in Much Wenlock, Shropshire.

Samantha Fernley is an online writer and keen church explorer with a background in ecology and volunteering for nature groups. She is based in Cheshire where she is involved in local heritage and church bell ringing.

Thomas Furly Forster (d. 1825) was a botanist who compiled many lists and drawings of plants. After his death, his natural history journals were collated and published by his son as *The Pocket Encyclopaedia of Natural Phenomena*.

Alexi Francis is an artist and illustrator living in Sussex. All her life she has been a lover of wildlife and studied zoology at university. She is interested in writing, especially about the natural world, and has had several articles published in anthologies and magazines such as *Earthlines*.

Jan Freedman is the curator of natural history at Plymouth City Museum and Art Gallery. Through writing and talks, he is very passionate about sharing the wonders and beauty of nature, both past and present. He runs a joint blog with two friends, opening a window into the magnificent world of Ice Age beasts. www.twilightbeasts.wordpress.com

Jennifer Garrett grew up in south-east London and has lived in Bristol for nine years. She works in communications and is interested in our engagement with nature in urban settings. She is also co-founder and chair of Bristol Nature Network, a popular group for 18–30s that offers free training to young naturalists, talks and film screenings, networking and social events.

John Green is the author of *Wings Over the Valley*, a lyrical account of a mid-Wales birdwatcher's experiences over several years, condensed into one year. It was nominated by *Guardian* readers as a classic of British nature writing. He is also the author of *In Search of Birds in Mid-Wales* and *Afon Ystwyth: The Story of a River*.

Caroline Greville is writing a book on her involvement with badgers in the context of her family life and wider rural setting. This memoir forms the main part of her PhD at the University of Kent, alongside research into new nature writing. She is Secretary of the East Kent Badger Group and teaches creative writing.

Sir Edward Grey (d. 1933) was a Liberal statesman, and the longest serving foreign secretary of the twentieth century (1905–16). He was also a keen ornithologist, and published *The Charm of Birds* in 1927, a record of his observations of birds and their song.

Vivienne Hambly is a writer and editor. She grew up in rural South Africa among hills writer Alan Paton described as being 'lovely beyond any singing of it'. Vivienne took a degree in geography and journalism at Rhodes University and is especially interested in the interactions between people and place. She lives in London.

Thomas Hardy (d. 1928) wrote several famous works including *Far from the Madding Crowd* (1874), *The Mayor of Casterbridge* (1886) and *Tess of the d'Urbervilles* (1891). Rural society was a major theme in his books; most were set in the partly imagined region of Wessex, based largely on areas of south and southwest England.

Zach Haynes, age twelve, lives in the wonderful North Yorkshire countryside. From an early age he has loved getting outside and exploring. He'd like all young people to love nature and understand how important it is to look after it. As well as exploring the countryside for new species to learn about, Zach writes regular blog posts about nature, volunteering and his campaigning for nature.

W. H. Hudson (d. 1922) spent his early years exploring the Argentinian landscape and he wrote several romances which are imbued its magic and beauty. After moving to London he achieved fame with a number of books about British and Argentinian ornithology, and the English countryside, including *A Foot in England* (1909) and *A Shepherd's Life* (1910), which helped encourage the 'back to nature' movement in interwar Britain.

Leigh Hunt (d. 1859) was first known as a critic for the notorious *Examiner* newspaper, founded by his brother John. Both brothers served two years in prison after publishing scandalous (but true) details about the Prince Regent in 1813. Hunt was friends with Shelley and Keats (who he introduced to each other), and after release from prison became well known as a poet himself.

Richard Jefferies (d. 1887) was a nature writer of both essays and novels, inspired by his upbringing on a farm. His works include *The Amateur Poacher* (1879), *Round About a Great Estate* (1880), *Nature Near London* (1883) and *The Life of the Fields* (1884). The collection *Field and Hedgerow* was published posthumously in 1889.

Ebenezer Jones (d. 1860) was born in Islington, London. His poetry was influenced by Thomas Carlyle and P. B. Shelley, and was not critically successful in his lifetime. He became friends with Robert Browning and Gabriel Dante Rossetti, the latter being responsible for Jones's modest critical reappraisal ten years after his death, aged forty, from consumption.

Miles King is chief executive of charity People Need Nature, which promotes the value and need for nature in people's lives. Miles has worked in nature conservation for thirty years, leading the conservation work at Plantlife, The Grasslands Trust and Buglife. He is the co-author of *Arable Plants: A Field Guide* and *The Nature of God's Acre*.

Olivia Laing is the widely acclaimed author of *To the River* (2011), shortlisted for the Ondaatje Prize and the Dolman Travel Book of the Year; *The Trip to Echo Pond* (2013), about writers and alcoholism, which was shortlisted for the Costa Prize; and *The Lonely City* (2016).

R. F. Langley (d. 2011) spent much of his adult life as a secondary school teacher and published most of his poetry in the final decade or so of his life, being nominated for a Whitbread Award for his *Collected Poems* (2000). His poetry was largely inspired by the Suffolk countryside where he spent his final years. In 2011 he won the Forward Prize for best single poem, for 'To a Nightingale'.

Philip Larkin (d. 1985) was a poet and novelist, best known for his poetry collections including *The Less Deceived* (1955), *The Whitsun Weddings* (1964) and *High Windows* (1974). He was the recipient of many honours, including the Queen's Gold Medal for Poetry in 1965.

Laurie Lee MBE (d. 1997) wrote a trilogy which taken together is one of the most famous autobiographies in British literature: *Cider With Rosie* (1959), *As I Walked Out One Midsummer Morning* (1969) and *A Moment of War* (1991). He died in his childhood village of Slad, Gloucestershire, which he had written about so famously in *Cider With Rosie*.

Clare Leighton (d. 1989) was an artist, writer and illustrator famous for her work depicting scenes of rural life. Her best-known works include *The Farmer's Year: A Calendar of English Husbandry* (1933) and *Four Hedges: A Gardener's Chronicle* (1935).

Georgia Locock is a seventeen-year-old naturalist and blogger who lives in Staffordshire. She enjoys nothing more than spending time exploring her patch then sharing her experiences through blogging in the hope of inspiring others. She is also a keen urban wildlife watcher, mammal watcher, and spends time encouraging those her own age and younger to love their natural surroundings.

Norman MacCaig OBE (d. 1996) was a prolific poet who divided his time between the West Highlands and Edinburgh, and whose poetry was acclaimed for its clarity and humour. He was uninterested in fashionable literary movements and undue reverence to the creative process, but was much admired by his peers.

Michael McCarthy has won a string of awards for his writing on the environment, first as Environment Correspondent of *The Times* and then as Environment Editor of the *Independent*. He is the author of *Say Goodbye To The Cuckoo* (2009), a study of Britain's declining summer migrant birds, and of *The Moth Snowstorm – Nature and Joy* (2015), both of which were widely praised.

Lucy McRobert is the Nature Matters campaigns manager for The Wildlife Trusts. She has written for publications including *BBC Wildlife*, is a columnist for *Birdwatch* magazine and was the Researcher on Tony Juniper's *What Nature Does for Britain* (2015). She is the creative director of A Focus On Nature, the youth nature network, and is a keen birdwatcher and mammal-watcher.

William Morris (d. 1896) was a poet, novelist and translator but is best known as textile designer and key figure in the Victorian 'Arts and Crafts' movement. The textiles manufacturing company he founded with his friends Gabriel Dante Rossetti, Edward Burne-Jones and others, proved hugely influential over Victorian interior design in the UK and America. He was also an early pioneer of socialism.

Emma Oldham has grown up with a notepad in one hand and some type of wildlife in the other. Spending many years in the field and graduating as a conservation biologist, Emma has blogged and documented her surroundings from a very early age. She is particularly motivated in engaging younger audiences, helping them make sure that nature doesn't drop off their agenda.

Alice Oswald is an English poet who was educated at New College, Oxford and now lives in Devon. She has published six collections of poetry and been the recipient of many awards, including the T.S. Eliot Prize in 2002 for her collection *Dart*, a work which looks at the River Dart in Devon through multiple perspectives.

Alexandra Pearce originally studied Marine Science before working as a zookeeper. A love of nature and a desire to tackle animal-related issues at the root of the problem led her to writing voluntarily for The Wildlife Trusts. Through this, Alex fell in love with educating people via the written word and now writes for a variety of charities, websites and magazines.

Megan Shersby is a naturalist and keen moth-trapper living in Cambridgeshire. She is a committee member of A Focus On Nature, Britain's youth nature network. Her wildlife blog (mshersby.wordpress.com) came Highly Commended in the BBC *Wildlife* magazine's Wildlife Bloggers Award 2015, and she has also written for local Wildlife Trusts, the Moths Count project and the Mammals in a Sustainable Environment project.

Edward Step (d. 1931) was the author of numerous books on nature, both popular and specialist, including *Favourite Flowers of the Garden and Greenhouse* (1896), *The Romance of Wild Flowers* (1901), *Nature in the Garden* (1910) and *Nature Rambles: An Introduction to Country-lore* (1930).

Edward Thomas' (d. 1917) works were often noted for his portrayals of the English countryside, including *In Pursuit of Spring* (1914), *The Heart of England* (1906) and *The South Country* (1909). Also known for his war poetry, he was killed during the First World War.

John Tyler has worked in nature conservation for many years, most recently as the Warden of the Sevenoaks Wildlife Reserve in Kent. He has a particular fondness for glow-worms and coracles. www.johntyler.co.uk

Julia Wallis, now semi-retired, takes great pleasure in creative writing. Although poetry calls loudest, she is also drawn to nature writing and has her first novel under way. Living on the edge of the countryside and helping out on a Midlands smallholding, she is never short of inspiration. Writing jostles for time alongside beekeeping, spinning and a plethora of country crafts.

Mary Webb (d. 1927) wrote romantic fiction largely set in her native Shropshire. Soon after her death aged forty-six, an endorsement from British Prime Minister Stanley Baldwin caused a surge in the popularity of her works, which prompted Stella Gibbons to satirise them in *Cold Comfort Farm* (1932). Her novel *Gone to Earth* was made into a film by Powell and Pressburger in 1950.

Reverend Gilbert White (d. 1793) was a curate, as well as a keen naturalist and ornithologist. His best known work is *The Natural History and Antiquities of Selborne* (1789), which has never been out of print; his journals were published posthumously, in 1931. He is considered by many to have been a major influence in forming modern attitudes to and respect for nature.

Matt Adam Williams is a conservationist, photographer and writer. He's Associate Director of A Focus on Nature, the youth nature network, and he works on climate policy for RSPB. He previously helped set up the UK Youth Climate Coalition and also spent a year working in the jungles of Borneo. He studied English and French at Oxford University. Follow him @mattadamw.

Janet Willoner lives in North Yorkshire and has been passionate about nature since childhood. She studied and taught Natural Sciences, had a career as a landscape watercolourist and took up writing on retirement. She has always loved spending time in wild places, experiencing solitude and observing wildlife, all of which inspire her art and writing.

Esther Woolfson, author of *Corvus: A Life With Birds* and *Field Notes from A Hidden City*, was Artist in Residence at Aberdeen Centre for Environmental Sustainability and Writer in Residence at Hexham Book Festival. An Honorary Fellow in the Department of Anthropology at Aberdeen University, she is working on a new book about human attitudes towards the natural world.

Annie Worsley is a mother of four and grandmother living on a coastal croft in the remote Northwest Highlands of Scotland. A former academic who explored the relationships between humans and environments in diverse parts of the world, including Papua New Guinea, she now writes about nature, wildlife and landscape. She tries to paint the wild using words.

Alan Wright is Senior Campaigns and Communications Officer for the Wildlife Trust for Lancashire, Manchester and North Merseyside. He writes a weekly wildlife column in the *Manchester Evening News*, its associated weekly papers and *Lancashire* magazine. Alan has been at the Wildlife Trust for five years after thirty years in journalism. He lives on the edge of the West Pennine Moors.

Benjamin Zephaniah is a poet, writer, lyricist and musician, born and raised in the West Midlands. Famously writing and performing in a style that became known as Dub Poetry, his work has been influenced by Jamaican culture and what he calls 'street politics'. He has written numerous books for both children and adults, and has worked with organisations campaigning for human rights and animal rights. He has sixteen honorary doctorates.

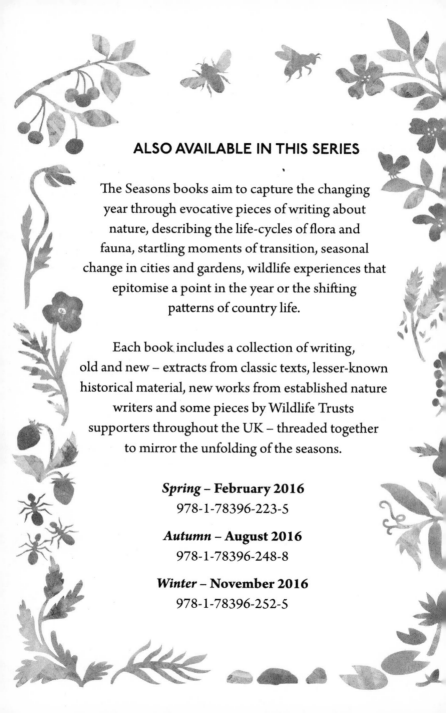

ALSO AVAILABLE IN THIS SERIES

The Seasons books aim to capture the changing
year through evocative pieces of writing about
nature, describing the life-cycles of flora and
fauna, startling moments of transition, seasonal
change in cities and gardens, wildlife experiences that
epitomise a point in the year or the shifting
patterns of country life.

Each book includes a collection of writing,
old and new – extracts from classic texts, lesser-known
historical material, new works from established nature
writers and some pieces by Wildlife Trusts
supporters throughout the UK – threaded together
to mirror the unfolding of the seasons.

Spring – **February 2016**
978-1-78396-223-5

Autumn – **August 2016**
978-1-78396-248-8

Winter – **November 2016**
978-1-78396-252-5